Ace Hudkins: Boxing With The Nebraska Wildcat

1Inscribed to the author's grandfather Conrad, "To Conie from Ace, your pal, wildcat."

Kristine Sader

"Had he [Ace] lived some eighty years earlier in Nebraska, he would have become a killer pure and simple, another Billy the Kid, perhaps, and would have died with his boots on and his skin full of lead. He was so tough and brutal in the ring that the late Commissioner Muldoon barred him from the New York rings simply because he was everything that a prizefighter should be."

Baker, George. "Ace Hudkins had the face of a killer." Boxing Illustrated: The Magazine for ring fans. March, 1961.

Copyright © 2018 by Kristine Sader
All rights reserved. This book or any portion thereof
may not be reproduced or used in any manner whatsoever without the express written permission of the publisher except for the use of brief quotations in a book review.

Printed in the United States of America

First Printing, 2018

ISBN 978-1-7328529-0-7

Dedicated with love to my Mom and Dad, Jean and Gene.

To Dad, for having the family with a story to tell, and to Mom, for encouraging me to tell it, and being with me every step of the long way. Love you.

Ace Hudkins: Boxing with the Nebraska Wildcat
Table of Contents

Introduction

The Nebraska Wildcat is Set Loose and Chicago Explodes!

1921: From the Y.M.C.A. to Turning Pro.

1924: California Meets The Wildcat!

1925: The Wildcat Meets The Latin Lover.

    The Wildcat Versus The Hollywood Sheik, Joe Benjamin

    The Role Of Cockiness as A Fighters' Tool

    The Wildcat and The Latin Lover, Valentino!

    The Olympic Auditorium and

    The Hollywood Legion   Stadium

1926: Ruby Goldstein and Coney Island, East Meets West.

1927: Lucky Lindy and The Wildcat!

    The Wildcat Vs. Sgt. Sammy Baker, The Bloodiest Fight Ever Seen!

    Joe Dundee Vs. Hudkins The Fight That Never Was

1928: The First Walker / Hudkins Fight, What Happened?

1929: Mickey Walker Vs. Ace Hudkins:

    The Black Tuesday Rematch.

Acknowledgements

Fight Record

Bibliography

Introduction

Home. Family. Brothers. The words are deeply ingrained in our collective memories, conjuring up images of a place; a warmth and a feeling of community, loyalty, even secrecy, that cannot be duplicated outside of their walls. At the turn of the century it was felt even more so, as families depended on each other for their daily livelihoods.

In the rural land of Nebraska, where the family home was located, seven brothers grew up not only supporting each other's dreams, but making one another's dream their own, and, literally, fighting fiercely to make those dreams a reality. It was imperative in this time and place, early 20th century Nebraska, that families could rely on each other financially as well as emotionally. This dependence and loyalty bound the brothers together so tightly, in good times and bad, that the family grip never loosened throughout their lives, and even beyond.

This bond even extended to their friends, who became "extended family." Time and again, they supported each other, bailed each other out, and stood by each other, keeping intensely guarded secrets within the family. Secrets that shaped this impenetrable bond that have never been broken even to this day, amongst family and co-workers, who speak with utmost respect and admiration of the "Hudkins Brothers Gang."

In order to understand the tightness of this bond it is important to remember where the Hudkins came from; and this is where the story of Ace, Clyde and Art begins.

From Hometown, Nebraska to Hollywood and Beyond

Like many little towns across America at this time, many Nebraskans, as proud as they might be of their hometown, decided to leave for something bigger. Something they may not have even been able to put a name on. As we travel through the state of Nebraska in the latter part of the 19th and the early part of the 20th century we encounter so many faces, many of whom will shape the entertainment, politics, and history of the 20th century. Is that little Hoot Gibson, pretending to be a cowboy? Who knew that he would move to California and become one of the biggest Western Cowboy stars of the 1920's? Perhaps we can stop by the Burwood or World Vaudeville Theaters or watch that Fred and Adele Astaire. Wow! Can they dance! They are making such a hit, that it won't be long until they move to California too, and Fred Astaire becomes the most popular dancer on the silver screen.

2 Scotts Bluff, Nebraska as it appeared in the 1950's. Photo by the Sader family. (Author's collection)

Then there is this young man in Norfolk, an amateur magician named John Carson, who they say is a pretty clever fellow. There is also this kid over in Lincoln name Dick Cavett who says he is going to Yale. Wouldn't it be something if down the line Johnny and Dick could meet up again with people like Fred Astaire, and maybe ask them a few questions?

But there are more and more folks moving to California in the 1920's and 30's: People like Ward Bond, who was born in Nebraska but grew up in Colorado, and the great Producer Daryl F. Zanuck. (They would meet the Hudkins later on for sure!) In the world of sports, Max Baer, Nebraska-born boxing World Heavyweight Champion, showed the world what Nebraskans could do, and Gorgeous George the famous, flamboyant wrestler, demonstrated style and showmanship.

The little Nebraska-born comedian and actor Harold Lloyd, famous for his film <u>Safety Last</u>, would live in Denver before moving to California in High School. But there were others, such as Robert Taylor, who attended Pomona College, Henry Fonda (An Omaha Community Playhouse graduate), Montgomery Clift and Marlon Brando all searched out the life of an actor, all ending up in Hollywood, a long way from Nebraska in those days.

Was it the example of Hoot Gibson, Fred Astaire, Ward Bond or Daryl F. Zanuck, men striking out and leading the way west, that gave the brothers the courage to go? Or was it born in their Nebraskan souls, like the wide plains and railroads, to wander, seek, and conquer? Why did some brothers leave and some stay? We may not answer all of these questions, but we will look and wonder, and maybe get a little bit of insight into the American spirit along the way. Although our story starts in place called Nebraska, and in a time when America was about to roar, first we need to check in with 22-year-old Ace and see what he was up to on a certain night in 1928.

"And if Hollywood wants a sure-fire script for a true-to-life movie, they should film the Ace Hudkins Story."

        Jim Raglin, *Lincoln Evening Journal*
        (Lincoln, Nebraska) 9 August 1955

The Nebraska Wildcat Is Set Loose, and Chicago Explodes!

The bell rang… the fight was brutal… the Wildcat was stunned… and the Toy Bulldog had won by a decision after ten rounds. The rain poured and the sound of 30,000 Chicago fight fans, most booing the decision, but some applauding it, nearly caused a rioting mob of outraged fans. It had taken Ace Hudkins a lifetime for the 22-year old to get to Chicago on Thursday June 21, 1928, and now it amounted to a split decision- a tie. Ace's brother, and manager, Clyde, speculated, "It was the dirtiest, rottenest, most insane decision ever rendered in the ring."

It was supposed to be a definitive knock-out: the "Nebraska Wildcat," Ace Hudkins, against the Middleweight Champion, Mickey Walker, the "Toy Bulldog", - after all, Ace was the main attraction here. In all his prior fights, both in Chicago and New York, Walker had never drawn over one hundred thousand dollars, yet due to Ace's popularity this fight was to bring in between one hundred fifty thousand and two hundred thousand dollars. At least a thousand fans from Nebraska, and likely many more, took a special train to Chicago just to see Ace. Although he wasn't knocked out- Ace had *never* been knocked out- he was still shaken. He'd thought it would be as easy as any other fight. Just like when he was a boy…just like back in Nebraska…

Ace, Clyde, and Art took The Gold Coast Limited from Nebraska to Hollywood, California. As the train sways and races along, Ace looks out the window and wonders, "How did I get here?" This thought was swiftly followed by the question, "What comes next?"

3 Ticket from the Mickey Walker - Ace Hudkins Match for the Middleweight Championship Of The World 1928

Beautiful Nebraska

4 Crayon and pencil on paper drawings by future sister-in-law to the Hudkins and Lincoln resident Marie Steinbrecker, 3rd grade, 1918. Most likely native birds she would have seen or the Nebraska state bird, The Western Meadowlark. (Author's collection)

For a moment, let's go back with Ace and see how it all began. Nebraska has a rich history and growing up there surely shaped the lives of the Hudkins brothers.

5 Farm life in Nebraska in the early to mid-20th century. Photo by the Sader family. (Author's collection)

John Hudkins was born in Virginia in 1856. John was a livery man – nobody living in Nebraska in the 1900's was afraid of hard work, and perhaps, his employment choice was a foretelling of how his sons would also work with horses. John wed Mary Mitchell, born in Illinois in 1866, and together John and Mary had nine children: eight boys and one girl: John Ira (Ira) (1882-1936), Willie (1885-1905), Alphonso (Fon) (1887- 1944), Katharine (Katy) (1888-1920), Oraine (Ode) (1892- 1967), Clyde (1894 -1969), Albert (Ab) (1897-1948), Asa (Ace) (1905-1973)   and Arthur (Art) (1907-1948).

In 1909, at the age of 53, John was found dead on the side of the road- he had had a stroke and been thrown from his horse. A woman left a widow at this time had very limited choices and it was up to the children to help support their mother any way they could. It must have been a rough job for a mother to raise a houseful of rambunctious boys who all needed a father's guidance. If they were full of spirit before his death, they ran wild after.

In June of 1915, 21-year old Clyde and a girlfriend were brought in by the police for being on the porch of an abandoned house. *"Both defendants testified that they were on their way home and had stopped on the porch to drink some pop that the girl had bought."* The charges were dismissed. In February of 1916, 29-year old Alfonso was arrested for fighting in a pool hall. In April of that year, he filed for divorce against his wife, claiming that she was consorting with people of bad character. He asked for care, or support, for his daughter. Alfonso and Myrtle were still married as of 1920 according to the census records, so it is possible that they reconciled or stayed together for the good of the daughter.

There were also dangers inherent in their professions at the time. In 1915, John Ira attempted to sue the city for $25,000.00 when, while working as a lineman in December of 1914, he was knocked off a telephone pole and rendered unable to work. He had been inspecting telephone wires and came into contact with electrical wires he claimed were too close to the telephone lines. He was thrown 15 feet. The non-insulated electrical wires were beneath the phone wires, so he had to climb over them both going up and down. The city council responded that they were not responsible. In 1917 John Ira, now known as Ira, got into a fight with a streetcar conductor, and hit him with a key. He was fined $10.00 plus costs. He filed for bankruptcy in 1921.

Becoming a fireman then, as now, was a dangerous and heroic occupation. Alfonso, or Fon, became a fireman- a junior captain at Havelock No. 4 Fire Station. He received burns while fighting a fire at the Evangelical Lutheran Church in 1925 while working for the Lincoln Fire Department. Alfonso was also a pitcher for the Denver Red Sox. Here, the Hudkins family mirrors American history, as baseball was becoming the "Great American Pastime." He passed away in 1944.

6 A Baseball Team in Lincoln, Nebraska, with Manager Henry Sader, and Conrad Sader , bottom row, second from right, Brother-in-law to Clyde Hudkins. Alfonso also played baseball quite successfully, for the Denver Red Sox. (Author's collection)

Ode also began work as a fireman in 1917. In July of 1920, he was badly burned fighting a fire located in a peanut factory when an electrical short circuit set plaster on fire, which then reached a twenty-five gallon oil container. *"Fireman Hudkins was in a second story window directing a stream of water on the flames when the oil exploded, throwing flames and burning gas twenty feet out of the window. He was badly burned about the head, shoulders, and hands."* The Lincoln Star (Lincoln, Nebraska) 21 July, 1920 page 8.

The Burlington and Missouri River Railroad

7 A 1919 postcard showing the Burlington Depot, published by the Acmegraph Co., Chicago

June 26, 1870 saw the Burlington and Missouri Railroad pull into Lincoln, followed by Midland Pacific and the Atchison and Nebraska in 1871 and '72. Let's see we would have experienced if we could stroll on down to the Burlington railroad yard in Lincoln in the early part of the 20th century!

The trains were ever rumbling through Lincoln. The Burlington Depot was alive with movement: people were bustling, steam shooshing, and above it all the loud voices of men giving information or instructions to one another. The railroad was life- and what more exciting way to live than working the rails? It was, after all, movement, activity, danger and freedom. At the railyard one was not on a farm, but in the thick of a new, thrilling world. The pastoral, natural, beauty of the plains, replaced by the modern, mechanical beauty of grease and engines.

Three of the brothers were employed by the railroad: William, until he died of Spinal Meningitis and Typhoid Fever at 19 years of age, in 1905. He started showing symptoms on a Monday, and passed away on Friday.

After his accident as a lineman, John Ira obtained work as a railroad switchman in 1925, and was there for nine years until he passed away in 1936, at the age of 53, still an employee of Burlington Railroad. He was also a member of The Brotherhood Of Railroad Trains. He had six daughters and four sons, two of whom, John Jr. (Bear) and Dick (Pee-wee), went on to work in movies as stuntmen and character actors.

Alfonso worked as an assistant yardmaster in the C. B. & Q. Railroad yards in Alliance, as well as being a fireman.

Germans From Russia

Germans had been enticed to the Volga region of Russia by promises of freedom and the opportunity to be free from military service. However, by 1873, political climates changed in Russia, and the Germans were looking at being conscripted into the Russian army. More and more Germans from Russia settled in the "North Bottoms," of Lincoln,

Nebraska and the surrounding areas. Clyde Hudkins married into a "Germans from Russia" family when he married Katherine Sader.

In a book entitled, *"My Antonia"*, by Willa Cather, we see a portrait of these hard working, free-spirited people: A people almost as free-spirited as the land itself. Here is an example from that book of how a child might have seen the prairie:

"I can remember exactly how the country looked to me as I walked beside my grandmother along the faint wagon-tracks on that early September morning. Perhaps the glide of long railway travel was still with me, for more than anything else I felt motion in the landscape; in the fresh easy-blowing morning wind, and in the earth itself, as if the shaggy grass were a sort of loose hide, and underneath it herds of wild buffalo were galloping, galloping..."

Buffalo Bill Cody

Next, if we were in Nebraska during the 1890's, we could stop in and see the great Buffalo Bill Cody, in Buffalo Bill's Wild West, a show he created in North Platte. He may not have been born in Nebraska, but there is little doubt that he was welcomed there as one of their own. We would have seen the horses and wagons flashing by as if on fire. We would have seen Native Americans dance, bending and rising in their traditional costumes, of bead and feathers, as the ground shook with their chant. We would have heard and felt the guns pop, we would have heard and felt the galloping hoofs of the horses thundering, thundering...

And there would stand the man himself, flowing hair, large-brimmed hat, bowing from his horse, ever the showman, Buffalo Bill!

Nebraska State Journal, November 12, 1893:

"North Platte people are proud of Buffalo Bill, proud of his world-wide reputation as a showman, proud of his ability to make money, and proud of the fact that Bill loves his home town and spends a great deal of his money here. His neighbors and friends delight to do him honor when he makes his appearance among them, and therefore when it became known that Cody would reach home Thursday night of this week preparations were at once made for a banquet at Lloyd's opera house Friday night, where he could be warmly welcomed by his many friends. There is no other place in the city large enough to accommodate Cody's North Platte friends and the opera house, which comfortably seats about fifteen hundred, was none too large last night . . .

Bill was there with his flowing hair, which is somewhat decorated with silvery threads, for age is beginning to tell on him. His tall form, graceful bow and hearty handshake attracted more attention than the food and flowers upon the table. He was happy to find his friends waiting for his coming, and the right royal welcome tendered him was gracefully received and duly appreciated.

This honor to Cody by his home people is perfectly proper, for no man has done as much for North Platte as he, and if he carries out to completion the enterprise he has planned for improvements here the coming year, much of the money he has earned in Chicago with his Wild West show [at the World's Columbian Exposition in 1893] will be used in building up and beautifying this portion of the state. He has just put about $15,000 in a beautiful residence and fine barn erected in the city this year and intends next spring to divide his large ranch property adjoining the city into eighty acre farms, build good improvements on each tract, procure good farmers and furnish them water for irrigating purposes...

The large two-story tallyho coach Bill brought from Chicago with him attracted more attention on the streets today than would a herd of buffalo or a band of

Sioux Indians. All citizens will now be treated to a tallyho ride, for Bill is always free with his favors and never stingy with anything."

Teddy Roosevelt

In 1900, we would have listened to a brash 42 yr. old Governor, and future President, the gallant Rough Rider, Theodore Roosevelt, speaking from Omaha at the completion of a tour of Nebraska:

"*I shall always remember Nebraska and her people*," said Governor Roosevelt in speaking of his tour, "*with favor and kindness. The cordial and respectful manner in which I have been greeted will ever remain a pleasant memory to me.*" The North Platte Semi-Weekly Tribune (North Platte, Nebraska) Friday, Oct 19, 1900.

Boys Town

8 Father Flanagan Statue at Boys Town taken in 1959. (Author's collection)

Now we need to take a tour of Father Edward J. Flanagan's Boys Town, opened in 1917, which gave a home and a purpose to homeless and struggling youngsters, some of whom would surely have been headed to prison without this special place in Omaha. As Father Flanagan said, *"There are no bad boys. There is only bad environment, bad training, bad example, bad thinking."*

9 Ace at approximately the same time that Boys Town was opening. William Jennings Bryan was the 41st United States Secretary of State. He was also a participant in the Scopes Monkey Trial in 1925 as an anti-evolution witness. In addition, he toured giving lectures on Christianity. (Clipping from Ace Hudkins' scrapbook.)

Ace worked as a "Newsie," selling newspapers for the Lincoln Journal when he was a youngster, a vocation that was dramatized in the movie and sage productions of <u>Newsies</u>. He was good at it. By 1922, he was selling more papers than the other boys and had to fight to keep his corner! It was a rough business for many youngsters, as each one was earning much needed money. In later years he would attend the annual Thanksgiving Dinner fundraiser given for the "Newsies" by the Los Angeles Newsboys Athletic Club, where he would box Mushy Callahan and others to raise funds for the newsboys.

Because Ace worked as a newsie, we will find little "Extra" news stories sprinkled throughout this book. You will know you've found one when you see the alert "Extra! Extra!," which was just the way Ace would have alerted people to important editions of his Lincoln Journal.

<u>The Union Airport</u>

Northeast of Lincoln, the Union Airport was opened in 1920, with the Lincoln Flying School at 2145 O Street able to boast Charles Lindbergh as their star pupil in 1922. The Municipal Airfield was named and dedicated to Charles Lindbergh in 1930, but that name did not last long as there was already another airfield so named in California.

If we happened to be around in February of 1922, we might have seen Charles Lindbergh practicing his flying skills in Lincoln. We would have heard the roar of the propeller and marveled as the craft lifted off the earth! "Lucky Lindy" would later cross paths with Ace Hudkins, with interesting results.

Extra! Extra! The Statue of Liberty in Nebraska!

10 Statue of Liberty replica in Scott's Bluff, Nebraska, taken by the Sader family. (Author's collection)

The Hudkins were as patriotic as the state they came from. Nebraska has been and continues to be a patriotic state. This Statue of Liberty Replica is in Scott's Bluff, Nebraska, at Pioneer Park 27th St. & Broadway. The plaque reads: *With the faith and courage of their forefathers who made possible the freedom of these United States, The Boy Scouts of America dedicate this replica of the Statue of Liberty as a pledge of everlasting fidelity and loyalty. 40th anniversary (of the Boy Scouts)*

Crusade to Strengthen the Arm of Liberty 1950. 8 1/2 feet tall without the base, weighing 290 pounds.

1905

1905—The year for scientific advances, new towns springing up from deserts, and the year for some fantastic music! Songs like *"Give My Regards To Broadway"*, and, *"Yankee Doodle"* by George M. Cohan expressed America's proud and patriotic attitude. But there were other songs like, *"In My Merry Oldsmobile"* by Gus Edwards and Vincent P. Bryan which expressed the thrill of a new century and new inventions with lyrics like, *"Each day they "spoon" to the engines tune."* Meanwhile, other songs like *"The St. Louis Rag"* by Tom Turpin, attracted the younger generation who dreamt of a more exciting life than the farm could offer.

Looking back at 1905, there was a lot of activity going on! Theodore Roosevelt, who had visited Nebraska in the past, was sworn in as President, after serving a first term due to President McKinley's assassination. Meanwhile, Albert Einstein was busily working on his special theory of relativity. Over in Nevada, a little town called Las Vegas was founded, which Ace would visit later. The Wright brothers were busy making history, as they piloted the first plane to stay in the air for more than a half an hour. Oh, yeah, and on a summer day Ace Hudkins was born!

"Anyone who knows boxing, knows the exploits of Ace Hudkins. He was a real fighter."

Nat Fleischer, boxing historian and publisher of RING magazine.

A popular song of 1919 asked the question:

"How ya gonna keep 'em away from Broadway?
Jazzin around and paintin' the town
How ya gonna keep 'em away from harm, that's a mystery
They'll never want to see a rake or plow
And who the deuce can parleyvous a cow?
How ya gonna keep 'em down on the farm
After they've seen Paree'?"

11 How Ya Gonna Keep 'Em Down On the Farm (After They've Seen Paree?) Music by Walter Donaldson, Lyrics by Joe Young, Sam M. Lewis 1919. (Public Domain)

This song perfectly illustrates the pull of the big city, even if the Hudkins boys had never seen Paris. Just like many young men of the era, and many young men before and after them, they wanted to see and experience everything life had to show them. There is little doubt that the Hudkins brothers, especially Ace, felt the draw of "jazzin' around," and experiencing a more dramatic life than Lincoln could offer.

Ace was born in Valparaiso, Nebraska, on August 30, 1905. He was the seventh son, and as he and Art were the youngest, they sold papers to help support the family after their father died and they moved to Lincoln.

By June 5 of 1917, Clyde was married to Katherine Sader and working at the Carter Transport Company a storage and moving service in Lincoln.

12 Postcard of Clyde's workplace as it looked when he worked there. http://www.exploredowntown.org/go/seaton-and-lea-ironworks-building

By 1920, older brother Clyde 24, listed himself as a fireman. He was not yet a fight manager on the census, and he and his wife Katherine, 23, as well as brothers Ab, 22, Ace, 14 and Art, 12, were living with their mother and step-father in Lincoln, Nebraska. Ace himself was a product of being born at a place and at a time when young men were encouraged to work hard and improve their station in life through labor. Being outspoken, sometimes to the point of cockiness, might be looked upon as confidence- which was expected if you wanted to move beyond your current station in life. It was the same spirit that led cowboys to tame the wild west- that is, if you could back up your words with actions. If you worked hard, you would succeed, but you had to be driven, and strong, to go far.

Looking back at the newspapers and magazines of the 1920's, we see many examples- through Ace's own words, that his early life was a rehearsal for his boxing life. He was in his first fight at 10-years-old, and his older brother Clyde earned a dollar from it. After that incident, he started attending a local Lincoln Y.M.C.A. clean life class.

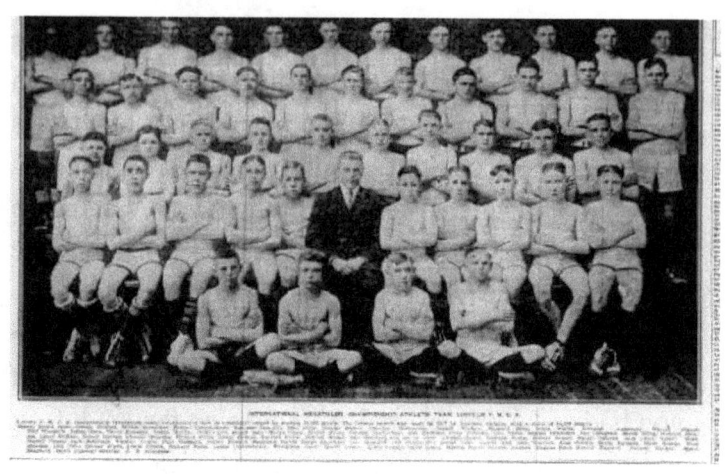

13 Ace in the International Hexathlon Championship Athletic Team 95 lb. Class. The hexathlon generally consists of 6 track & Field events: hurdles, long jump, javelin, high jump, shotput and 800 m.

There were many stories and articles printed about Ace's start in the ring. The truth seems to lie somewhere in-between the lines of each story that was told.

Ace started wrestling at 15- and we know that Conrad Sader, Clyde's brother-in-law, (Conrad's sister was Kathryn, Clyde's wife) encouraged him to try boxing at the local Y.M.C.A.

Charlie Moon, State Boxing Commissioner for Nebraska, also took credit for Ace joining the Y.M.C.A. *"He could have been a champ in one or more divisions if he had been handled properly. He sold Journals in front of my former business establishment when he was a scrawny kid of 10 or 12. I bought him a member ship in the Y.M.C.A. and he soon was the state champion in the 108-pound division. Then he turned to boxing and was the toughest man in the ring I ever saw.*" says Moon, in a 1955 Lincoln Evening Journal article.

Two Weeks To Beat The Champ

In one article - from a copy of Arena Magazine dated 1929, we read this account of Ace's start: "*It seems that Ace got into an argument with the Y.M.C.A. kids boxing champion. When the champ said, 'If you was a fighter, I'd show you,' Ace replied, 'I'll be a boxer in two weeks and you'll get a chance.'*" Two weeks later, Ace, true to his word, knocked out the Y.M.C.A. champ.

Another story, from the Lincoln Evening Journal from 1926, claims- "*Ace was a cocky 14-year-old working in a pool hall, and mouthing off, when local boxer Harold Jolsmer teased him saying, 'I wish you were a fighter so I could tame you with a few socks on the jaw.' The red-head spouted back, 'Maybe I don't need to be a fighter to whip you!'*" Well, two weeks later the young gun knocked out the local champ!

Whichever way it happened, it appears that Ace challenged the local champ, trained for a couple of weeks, then knocked down the biggest contender that he could find! This was true to his nature, as we shall see later. Ace always took on the champ to prove that he had the stuff to beat the best.

He Hated To Be Beaten-- That Was All!

According to interviews and articles from the '20s, "The Ace" was a champion at any sport he tried. The famous Hudkins' bond was also apparent as Ace insisted on including his younger brother Art in any sport he played, or having him included in any team he played. When the teams tried to coax him with, "c'mon and play Asa!" he always answered with, "Only if Art can play too!" This was nothing unusual for Ace - it was just part of being a brother.

The Lincoln Evening Journal, 1926 claims that Ace was sought after by all of the local sports clubs, baseball, football but- it didn't matter. Ace saw that his brother was being teased for being "the fat one", so he would only play if they allowed Art to play as well. This meant that Art was included and would get to play - and perhaps, pounded - but Ace would yell signals in the backfield, "with his red hair blazing around the right end."

This same article goes on to describe an incident demonstrating Ace's prowess in the water, as well as his stubborn nature, cockiness, and actual athletic ability. A powerful combination!

Of course, when a five-mile swim was held in the Blue River near Crete, Nebraska, Ace wanted in. Art (Ace's trainer), and Clyde (Ace's manager) paced him from a rowboat. The problem was, they couldn't keep Ace from talking- he just wouldn't keep his mouth shut. Once, he turned over onto his back and exclaimed, *"This is the easiest thing I ever did!"*. *"You'd better shut up and save your wind!"* they told him! During the last mile, the other contestants started to sprint, so naturally Ace sprang into action and left the pace boat with Art and Clyde behind him. He landed on the dock first—then he simply jumped back in to swim to his brothers and joined them in the boat. He also won recognition for a two-mile swim while at a Y.M.C.A. camp on the Blue River at Crete on July 4, 1920.

    Ace surely showed an aptitude for many sports, including cross-country racing, further illustrated in the same article. He just willed himself to succeed. Once, when he was 13, he entered a 12-mile municipal cross-country race. He ran, despite the fact that he had no experience in cross-country running, and came in, bleeding from being hit by brambles and scrambling over rocks.

Ace hated to be beaten. That was all.

14 He hated to be beaten, at anything! (Author's collection, photo by Clark)

Clearly, Ace was known as the brother with the physical and athletic ability as well as a pugnacious attitude. He simply would not give in and he would never give up. Clyde and Art both had their theatrical roles to play in this traveling pugilistic talent show. Clyde was the manager - he saw the opportunities and steered Ace toward them, while Art was the smooth talker and ladies' man.

Both Clyde and Art had one very important job in common, and it was natural, as well as obligatory: they would support and promote their brother. Art and Clyde would never miss an opportunity to tell the press how their brother was going to defeat this or that opponent.

Are these fantastic stories of Ace's early mastery of football, swimming, cross-country racing etc… absolutely factual? They could be, but who is to say? Did they make up these stories for the press, and for publicity- is that even important? The stories served to demonstrate two things that were undeniable and all too real: a family sticking together, and Ace's talent. The stories captivated readers and created a mystique around this unbeatable young man.

What we know for certain is that Ace had natural abilities, was on his way as a boxer, and his brothers were with him with one hundred percent devotion. At one point, they pooled together the seven dollars they'd earned by selling papers and bought Ace a wrestling uniform. There were other reasons, besides Ace's obvious physical gifts, to want to get out of Lincoln.

From 1920 to 1933 The United States was officially committed to Prohibition, the ban of the production, sale and transport of alcohol. Because of the ban, many began to make home-made alcohol, either for sale or to drink within the household. One family member (who chose to remain anonymous, demonstrating the loyalty that remains to this day) - stated, "*Before that* (the boxing), *they all run booze back there in Nebraska when they lived in Lincoln.*" The years that Prohibition lasted were prime years for young Ace, and he was always one to work hard at making a living. If not for boxing, it is unclear what path of employment would have lain ahead for rambunctious young Ace who never graduated High School, and later lamented, "*All I know is fighting. If I had stayed in school I could perhaps do something besides perform in that ring, but that's all too late now.*" In our opinion, and in the opinion of the many who came to see him battle, his performance in that ring was more than enough.

1921

From the Y.M.C.A. To Turning Pro!

Ace won the 108-pound Wrestling Championship of Nebraska. Pat Boyle, from Lincoln, watched Ace wrestle for five days at the Lincoln Y.M.C.A.

"'*What,' Boyle asked the boy, 'do you want to be when you grow up?'* ...

'I am grown up,' he retorted -in typical Ace fashion- *'and I'm going to be what I can make the most money at and get the most fun out of.'*

'That,' said Boyle approvingly, 'is a tall order. How'd you like to have some fun and make money-starting next week?'

Hudkins never batted an eyelash. 'Sure.'"

A chance to have fun and make money sounded pretty good to Ace!

Before Ace knew it, Boyle had arranged a fight for him, without training and with very little preparation. The larger opponent knocked Ace down and said, "*Get down and stay down, punk.*" At the count of 8, Ace jumped up and pounded the guy! Boyle told the kid that he was gonna be "*okay*"

Unfortunately, Boyle didn't work fast enough for the seven hungry Hudkins brothers, and they soon decided to separate, although neither side seems to have had hard feelings.

"'Ace,' said brother Clyde, the spokesman, 'you have it in you to be a great fighter.' Ace agreed, 'Sure, but Boyle is holding me down.'

'So,' said Clyde, 'we're going to make this a family affair. How about me being your manager and Art being your trainer? That way we can keep all the money in the family. Okay?'

It was okay with Ace- and so was born the famous triumvirate 'Ace, Deuce and Trey Hudkins,' another of boxing's great families."

So Ace made a couple of decisions: the first was to go professional with boxing, which would give him a life he could have only dreamt of as a young, extremely raucous, kid in Nebraska; the second was to release Boyle and keep the money in the family. This made all of the brothers' financial dreams come true, affording them the chance to move all the way from the Nebraska farms to the bright lights of Hollywood. They were set for life, but at that point, they didn't know it. Ace decided to make it a family business - the business of Ace Hudkins, The Nebraska Wildcat.

Extra! Extra!

Wrapping up 1921, let's see what is going on in the rest of the news. There is a sweet, touching movie out called *The Kid* which starred Charlie Chaplin and Jackie Coogan. If you are in the mood for music, there are some great popular songs out such as, *I Ain't Got Nobody, Ain't We Got Fun, Margie, Look For The Silver Lining, Avalon* and *Second Hand Rose.* The first Miss America Pageant is held, and Donna Reed and *Gilligan's Island's* Skipper Allen Hale Jr. are born. The Hudkins would work with the Skipper's dad, Allen Hale, years later at Warner Brothers Studio.

1924
California Meets The Wildcat!

Nineteen – year -old Ace won the Nebraska State Lightweight title on September 4th. The match took place in the City Auditorium in Lincoln, Nebraska. Harry Reed was the referee. Ace Hudkins vs. Kid Worley! Ace was primed and won by a knock out in the 9th round, thereby taking the title and proving his ability. He could now move up the ladder to more established opponents.

Ace had to decide. Should he stay in Nebraska, continuing to beat everyone he fought? He was the best there, sure, but could he make it in the big time? Could he beat the best of the best, and how would he prove it by staying in Nebraska and not challenging himself? Ace was always looking ahead, his sights set on the big time- in other words- Hollywood! There was a reason that the song *"California, Here I Come"* was a big hit. Al Jolson introduced the song in 1921 and recorded it in 1924 so it couldn't be coincidence that Ace was drawn to Hollywood, California during that same year.

Hollywood in the 1920's was as fast and loose as a town could be: the traffic, the excitement, and the new "screen stars!" Let's not forget that boxing was big in both California and New York. Not to mention that the image of boxing in the California sunshine, with palm trees waving in the background and starlets abundant, was probably preferable to the image of the traffic and crowds of New York. Clyde and Ace hit Los Angeles with $2.00 to spare!

"*Meet the Nebraska Wildcat!*" *The Arena,* Oct 10, 1929:

> "*A trip to Hollywood would mean ruination to most fighters, but to Ace Hudkins, cornfed Nebraska boy, it was the "makings." Hudkins...started on the road to fame and fortune the night he made his first appearance at the Hollywood Legion Stadium. At that Hudkins had to beg for his chance at Hollywood, which is not unlike the stories of countless others who have stormed the Film City searching for a start in the motion picture industry.*
>
> *Hudkins and his brother Clyde arrived in California almost penniless. He hit Hollywood and struck it rich almost from the start. But that start only came after the Hudkins boys had walked the streets haunting the offices of the boxing moguls in and around Los Angeles.*"

In November of 1924, Ace and Clyde strutted the streets of Hollywood visiting this gym, and that gym, and it helped that Ace had the looks of a young Spencer Tracy mixed with the swagger of James Cagney. Such was their manner when they waltzed in to Kaufman's Gym in Hollywood. This was it! It smelled right, and it felt right. This was definitely the place! If they were going to properly introduce themselves to Hollywood, there was no better location, and no better time than now.

The two brothers knew exactly what had to be done. Nobody was going to give Ace a chance based solely on the fact that he had been successful back home, no matter how many fights he had won, and no matter that he had never been knocked out. For the boxing community to accept Ace, they had to see it with their own eyes.

It is worth noting that there was no "social media" per se at this time. No instant fame from a homemade video. With social media today, one could look on a phone or tablet and see film of him boxing. Back then, they were not about to take this brash kid's word for it - he had to prove it. It was "show me" time.

But Ace was never one to shy away from hard work to show what he could do. He had the guts, and he had his brother with him. He offered to box anyone present and soon found himself up against Joe Dunn, a 148-pound boxer! Ace won there and then; both the match and the respect of all who witnessed this exhibition.

By December, Ace and Clyde were still pounding the pavement, going from gym to gym making a name for themselves, but it looked like it was shaping up to be a cold Christmas, even in sunny Hollywood. Tom Kennedy was the matchmaker for Hollywood at that time. Boxer, Dick Hoppe was scheduled to fight an Eastern lightweight, and it happened that the opponent sprained his ankle only two days before the fight. Who could Kennedy get on that short of a notice? In his note book, he found Hudkins' name and decided that any fighter that would take on Hoppe on two days' notice, must have the stuff. Ace recalled this experience in this interview in *The Arena Magazine* from 1929:

> *"Things have changed a lot since I first came to California...Clyde and I were flat broke, and we were considering going out and digging ditches or something, when Kennedy offered me that chance at Dick Hoppe. Believe me, it was a chance too.*
>
> *I knew that under ordinary circumstances I could beat Hoppe or anybody else they gave me. But we were so broke, and eating so irregularly, that I didn't know*

whether I'd be able to get in there and punch with him. I didn't have to train to get my weight down or anything. I was down to darn near the featherweight class, I was so hungry."

On December 19, 1924, Ace fought the expert boxer, Dick Hoppe, in his first fight at the Hollywood Legion Stadium. He not only fought- he WON! By the end of the night, Ace had 116 points, and Hoppe had 85. It was an early Christmas for the Hudkins family. Ace earned $500.00 for the fight, a large portion of which went home to Nebraska. However, they went to bed hungry the night of the fight and had to wait until 11 o'clock the next morning to eat, as that was when Kennedy paid them.

Extra! Extra!

As 1924 rolls into 1925, let's look back on that fascinating year! Chamonix hosted the winter Olympics, and George Gershwin's *Rhapsody In Blue* is performed. In other news, J. Edgar Hoover is named head of the Federal Bureau of Investigation, and Robert Horton of t.v.'s *Wagon Train* is born. Later, Rich Brehm, nephew of the Hudkins, would be the head wrangler on *Wagon Train.*

1925

The Wildcat Meets The Latin Lover!

January 10, 1925

Ace fought Tommy Carter at The Hollywood Legion.

This was the first important ten- round fight in Southern California. The crowd was packed in and Adam Walsh was introduced before the game as, "Notre Dame's great halfback," and presented with a gold wristwatch from the Hollywood Legion. During the sixth round, Ace caught Carter's chin with a series of right and left hooks until, finally, a right cross knocked him down for a count of nine.

However, all of those sixth-round blows cost Ace. The next day he found out that he had broken his right hand during that all-important sixth round. Knowing the Ace as we do, he couldn't just win, he'd done it by fighting four rounds with a broken hand and earned himself the Pacific Coast Lightweight Title.

The Wildcat versus The Hollywood Sheik

There were two sheiks in Hollywood during the 1920's, and Ace met both of them. The first was Joe Benjamin, variously known as "The Hollywood Sheik," or "The Sheik from Stockton." The second was the world-famous Latin lover and heartthrob,

Rudolph Valentino, simply known as "The Sheik," having been named after his most famous movie role.

April 7, 1925

One of the ways Ace prepared for his bout with Joe Benjamin was by sparring with Jackie Fields at The Newsboy's Club. Both Ace and Joe Benjamin had their own personal feelings about each other. Joe Benjamin, "The Sheik From Stockton," was sore at Hudkins because after he'd fought Jack Silver in San Francisco, Ace said that he could beat them both on the same day. Meanwhile, Hudkins was sore at Benjamin because Benjamin dictated the weigh-in weight at 137 pounds, whereas Ace wanted to weigh in at the regular lightweight limit of 135 so that the bout would be recognized by the New York Commission. The winner of this match would have a good claim to the lightweight title vacated by Benny Leonard.

As trainers always did with Ace, then-trainer "Gig" Rooney did his best to keep him in line and get him to go to bed early the night before the fight. Whether he succeeded or not, Ace was in rare form the day of the fight.

Hudkins hit Benjamin in the stomach with a left like a rocket. In the sixth round, Ace's punches, culminating in vicious rights to the jaw and to the "sheik's" formerly-pretty face, closed his right eye and sent Benjamin first to the ropes, then to the floor. There was no count, but it had the desired effect- Benjamin lost his spirit after that.

Immediately after winning the bout, Hudkins was suspended from boxing in the state of Nebraska because Harry Reed, who had been Ace's previous manager for a time, claimed that Ace had violated his contract with him. Reed had sold the contract to Pat Boyle of Omaha. Boyle did not complete the settlement with Reed. Somewhat ironically, Benjamin was also suspended by the California Boxing Commission because he was injected with a pain killer for his hand during the bout. This proved to be Joe Benjamin's last professional bout, and three days later he hired (no doubt due to the rights in the face he suffered during the Hudkins fight) Dr. William Balsinger, a plastic surgeon who worked on Jack Dempsey and would work on Ace in the 1930's to repair his face.

After Ace beat both Tommy Carter and Benjamin, Clyde knew that his brother had to go East and match up with those fellas if he was going to be respected nationally. Ace had fought in Chicago before, beating Frankie Schaeffer in two out of three bouts. Now, they would return with more experience and a title under Ace's belt. Clyde wanted Ace to fight Sid Terris.

According to George Baker's article, "*Ace Hudkins Had The Face Of a Killer*," once in Chicago, reporters asked Ace who he had fought in order to earn his place fighting Terris. He answered,

" 'I licked Joe Benjamin, the best lightweight in California.' … One reporter said dead-pan, 'The best in California? We never heard of him here in Chicago.' And the Ace replied, 'No—but you're sure as h*** going t' hear about me!'"

Sid Terris was smart, and he avoided Ace in the ring at all costs, dancing around the ring, practically running from him, thereby winning the match. Afterwards, Terris commented, *"I'd have been a d***** fool to swap punches with that wildcat!"*

Before the Goldstein fight of 1926, Terris told Goldstein, *"Hudkins? Don't worry about him. Just stay on your horse. I kept away from him, and so can you. He's a slugger, but you, Ruby, have the punch. You'll knock him dead inside of five."* Would he? We'll see, later on.

The Wildcat and The Latin Lover

In 1925, one man's name could make women swoon, and men jealous. That name was Valentino. The term "Latin Lover" was created especially for him. As an actor, he usually portrayed strong men such as "Ahmed Ben Hassan", in *The Sheik*, and "Juan Gallardo", the matador, in *Blood and Sand*. It is impossible to overstate Valentino's appeal as a star of the screen, but he also played in costume dramas at the time, which made him appear slightly foppish.

"Foppish," was not the type of image that Rudolph Valentino wanted in real life- after all, he was the most popular male star of the "20's". To strengthen his masculine image after playing more sentimental romantic leads in "parlor dramas," such as *Monsieur Beaucaire*, Rudolph Valentino, the pre-eminent sex symbol of the 1920's big screen, took up boxing and boxing exhibitions. He was trained by Jack Dempsey himself and it was reported that Valentino wore something of a catcher's mask when boxing, to protect his face- he was a romantic symbol, after all, and couldn't risk damaging his features.

When the call came in asking Ace if he would like to spar with Valentino, we can only imagine his response. After all, publicity, and Hollywood stardom were two activities that Ace fully supported. Who better to train, and spar with the Latin Lover, than the Nebraska Wildcat?

15 Ace sparring with Rudolph Valentino.

The Best In the Ring met The Best On The Screen. The two greats were featured as of June 4th in *Grantland Rice's Sportlights*, a sports film which showed in theaters before the main feature film. Valentino wore no mask as he sparred with Hudkins.

Rudolph Valentino's boxing interest and skill are the talk of Hollywood. The picture shows him training with Ace Hudkins, Pacific Coast lightweight champion, who recently whipped Joe

Benjamin. Valentino has an excellent physique, extremely fast foot action and a wicked left jab. On the Pacific Coast, Hudkins is being touted as the next world's champion.[1]

When Rudolph Valentino died in August of 1926, at 31 years old, eighty-thousand fans attended his funeral. Women were in hysterics, and dozens of suicide attempts were reported.

Extra! Extra!

The Olympic and Hollywood Legion

From the article, "'*Ace' Hudkins Packs Them In At Hollywood*":

> "'*Ace' Hudkins, Nebraska fighter, is the big noise at Hollywood, Los Angeles suburban hub of the movie industry. Damon Runyon, New York scribe, is touring the coast country and writes as follows concerning the success of the mitten sport in Hollywood and the popularity of the Lincoln youth:*
>
>> *'Tex' Rickard would love a pugilistic business such as is enjoyed by the Hollywood arena. Any card is almost a sellout, because the show is almost incidental to the weekly gathering.*

---

[1] Back of photo quote.

Certain boxers will pack the place to the very doors. The present pugilistic rage of Hollywood is one Ace Hudkins, a lightweight from Nebraska. He could box this writer heaven forbid, and you couldn't find standing room.

The Hollywood 'ringworms' will tell you that Ace Hudkins-Ace is his real Christian name- is the next lightweight champion of the world. The writer is not so sure of that. However, he concedes that Hudkins is a good fighter.

He is a rugged, fighting fellow. He gives the crowd ACTION. That is what the Hollywood people crave.

They like the slam-bank, whoop-tee-doo style born of the four-round game. Scientific boxing doesn't appeal to them. The writer knows very few fistic fans who really prefer science to slugging.

The leading referee at the Hollywood arena is Larry McGrath, a former New York boxer...besides refereeing, McGrath also works on the pictures."

-Clipping from Ace Hudkins' Scrapbook

During this time, Ace was one of the top draws at places like Legion Stadium in Hollywood (also known as The Hollywood Legion Stadium), The Olympic Auditorium in Los Angeles, Vernon Arena and Ascot Park in Los Angeles working his way further and further up the sports ladder. Ace debuted at The Olympic on September 16, 1925, against Mushy Callahan. The auditorium opened in 1925, and soon the stars were out and sitting ringside. Stars such as Al Jolson, Ruby Keeler, and Mae West among others frequented The Olympic, while Jack Benny, Humphry Bogart, George Burns, Eddie Cantor, Errol Flynn, Clark Gable, Alan Hale, Bob Hope, Jolson, William Powell, George Raft, Mickey Rooney and Ann Sothern could be seen often, and even the Marx brothers clowned around, in the ring at the Hollywood Legion.

Gene LeBell, stuntman, and son of Olympic Auditorium icon Aileen Eaton, reminisced about The Olympic, and *Raging Bull*:

"My family had this boxing auditorium called the Olympic Auditorium. I knew him (Ace) just to talk to him. I never saw him fight, but he had a good reputation. Sometimes when you live on your reputation nobody wants to mess with you. Now a few of the guys used to come down to the Olympic, 'cause I could get free tickets 'cause my mother owned the place. These guys were all boxing fans. So they all went down, and I got them good

seats at the Olympic Auditorium, and that was a big thing. My mother had it for 38 years, and I narrated wrestling and sometimes boxing.

From the 50's on, I went every week to the fights. There are so many cowboys that used to go. Even Clint Eastwood used to go there. Wally Rose who was a stuntman, (Wally worked on Spartacus, Blazing Saddles, The Champ 1979, and many other great projects.) *he went there, but all these guys are gone. I probably shot a hundred movies up there. Rocky was there. Raging Bull was there.*

Well, I'll tell ya a funny thing there. I was the ring announcer during the big fight, (in Raging Bull) and you could see me and see what I look like, and the next day I was a fan with a mustache and a hat throwing chairs at myself! There was a riot (in the movie), *and myself was actually the camera! Kinda funny!"*

When asked about working with the director Martin Scorsese, Gene LeBell had this to say, *"Well, I'll tell ya what, a great man. The* (actual) *rings were 24 x 24, and they had this like 24 x 50* (movie set ring), *and I said, "That isn't the way it is." And he said, "Well, I gotta put the camera somewhere don't I?"*

He (Scorsese) *was nice to me. He wanted to know what color trunks they had during Maxim, that was the fighter they were doing, Joey Maxim. He wanted to know what kind of trunks he had and what color. So I go up to the secretary, her name was Shirley O Brien, and she looked it up in her archives, and he had purple pants on. She typed it up, and I gave it to him, and he gave me 500 dollars for doing it. I didn't ask for any money, I was just surprised! I said, "He was wearing purple trunks." He says, "That's nice." I said, "Are you gonna get purple trunks?" He said, "No, this is in black and white." If you notice it was in black and white. So, why did he want to know the color? I don't know. But it turned out De Niro got an Academy award for it."*

16 George Raft, Clyde Hudkins, Pat O'Brien and James J. Braddock, the "Cinderella Man", at the Hollywood Legion Stadium. Provided by Hollywood Legion Stadium Facebook Page Administrators.

Ace had his debut at The Hollywood Legion on December 19, 1924, winning against Dick Hoppe. There was also another figure in the audience: Mickey Cohen.

Although Ace was Nebraska State Lightweight Champion, and was well known in Los Angeles, he was not quite a national contender. He knew that he would have to go east and challenge the best on that coast to advance his reputation. Ruby Goldstein was then known as "The Jewel of The Ghetto", and that was who Ace wanted, and needed, to beat.

Extra! Extra!
The Role of Cockiness as a Fighter's Tool

Call it conceit. Call it cockiness. Call it bravado or bravery. Every long-careered, successful boxer has "it". They must. Imagine for a moment you are a gladiator waiting to enter the Colosseum. If you enter timidly, eyes down and fearful, you lose your edge, and are sure to be picked off. If, however, you enter shouting, "I am the best!", and "No one is better than me! Bring them on!", even if you don't believe it totally, you win before you ever begin to fight. You not only convince yourself, but your opponents. Did the great Muhammed Ali say, "I'm okay, I guess."? No! He said "I am the greatest. I said that even before I knew I was... I figured that if I said it enough, I would convince the world that I really was the greatest."

So it was with Ace "The Nebraska Wildcat" Hudkins. Though he and his brothers used different terminology, he was "the greatest" before Ali coined the term. Journalist Robert Edgren described Ace in this way in an article in October of 1925:

> "*On the pacific coast is a lightweight boxer who is making a fortune by his overwhelming conceit. ... he 'packs 'em in' every time he fights. Half the crowd goes to see Hudkins' antics in the ring, and the other half goes hoping to see him whipped...Hudkins has the self-confidence* (sic) *of a Los Angeles real estate agent...and a rapidly fattening bank account...absolutely certain that he's the cleverest boxer in the world...smiling at his own cleverness and talking constantly with clownish gestures and wide grins, inviting the other fellow to hit him... clowning, talking, swinging wildly... Wildness is his stock and trade. When given a draw, Hudkins throws his hands over his head and makes faces to show the crowd he thinks he's been robbed. Then he stands in the middle of the ring and pats himself on the chest, shakes hands with himself, congratulates himself for winning, grips his hands together over his head and goes*

through the motions of shaking hands with the crowd after which he (curtsies?) from side to side and bows smilingly in all directions. It makes the referee and the boxing commission look foolish, but it's great stuff for Hudkins. He's one of the best drawing cards in the west...Hudkins has only the agent's selling tricks."

Unfortunately, Ace's outspokenness led to fisticuffs outside of the ring on more than one occasion. Other fighters had been challenged in the barroom before, just to get their names mentioned in the paper, however Ace was different. Instead of walking away with a shrug, saying, "Nuts to you!", if Ace were slightly spiffed, (and being in a barroom, it was a likely condition), he would allow the civilian to take a swing, whereby the challenger would quickly regret their decision.

17 Ace working out, May 1925. Reproduced from the original held by the Department of Special Collections of the Hesburgh Libraries of Notre Dame.

Extra! Extra! 1925 Edition!

Mushy Callahan, Ace's two-time opponent on September 16, and November 14, 1925, went on to run a haberdashery in Los Angeles, then went to work for Warner Bros. Studios and others, training actors and actresses for roles involving prizefighting.

Henry Fonda used 1925 to decide that he wanted to make acting his career, starting off at The Omaha Playhouse at the recommendation of Doe Brando, Marlon's mom.

From The Police Gazette, Year Unknown

ACE HUDKINS
Born Aug. 30, 1905, Valparaiso, Neb. Weight, 145 pounds. Height, 5 ft. 8 in. Nationality—Irish-Scotch-American.

1926

Training With Ace

In the meantime, Ace waited to fight Ruby Goldstein, and he trained. He prepared and worked every day. Here is a sample of his training schedule, according to The Nebraska State Journal February, 1926:

> *"Hudkins climbs out of bed at 7 a.m. and goes on the road for 7 or 8 miles. Returns home for a rub down and then eats breakfast. He spends mornings around home learning the intricate steps of the Charleston, (his brother Clyde says he is getting good at this). Leaves home at noon to wrestle with the Lions at Bay's (sic…Gay's) lion farm. Gets to the gymnasium at 2 o'clock and works out until 4:30. Home to dinner of T-bone steak, lettuce, tomatoes and orange juice. Listens to the radio until 10 o'clock when he retires. He hasn't a girlfriend in Los Angeles."*

According to this article, Ace trains by running, dancing, and wrestling lions! Not only that, but he is single!

18 Ace "wrestling" a lion at Gay's Lion Farm in El Monte.
CA. Sueddeutsche Zeitung Photo / Alamy Stock Photo

He Likes His Car—but Doesn't Ride in It

19 Ace Hudkins thinks his Cadillac sedan is O.K., but there are times when he won't ride in it—as the photograph shows. That is when he is training. The "Cad" is ideal as a pacemaker and it isn't as hard on Ace's trainer. (Clipping from Ace Hudkins' Scrapbook)

20 One of Hudkins' cars. (Author's Collection)

"Out through Griffith Park every morning rolls a big Cadillac sedan. It travels at a moderate pace, for, contrary to custom, the owner of said sedan is not riding in it, but running alongside. Hudkins takes the five miles of road work through the park every morning when he is in training as he is at present for his forthcoming fight with Adams, and the Cadillac sets the pace." -The Los Angeles Times, April 11, 1926.

21 "The Three Aces: Ace, Deuce and Trey!" (Clipping from Hudkins' Scrapbook)

June 25

Ruby Goldstein

Coney Island Stadium, Brooklyn. 18,000 fans arrived ready to see a bout for the ages. Ace was a 4-1 underdog. Art and Clyde had practiced hand signals to coach Ace during the bout, even though the rules barred them from being too close to the corner. During the first round, Goldstein sent a right cross at Hudkins which in turn sent Hudkins down for a count of 1….2…3…4….5. Goldstein turned his back, thinking the fight was won. His manager, Hymie Caplan, started to point towards Ace. They couldn't believe it! The Wildcat got up again! Round two saw Goldstein ahead, and the third round was a draw. Round 4: Hudkins knocked Goldstein down twice, the second time with a left hook and a right cross straight to the jaw. As the count reached 10, 18-year-old Goldstein was still holding on to the rope as he was counted out. It took an hour to revive him. Hudkins had never been- and never would be- knocked out in his professional career.

"When Goldstein hit you, that was supposed to be it… but when Goldstein hit Hudkins, Hudkins not only didn't go down, he stood there growling and snarling at Goldstein. That's my kind of

fighter." Mike Tyson, Los Angeles Times, Jul 29, 1989

Ruby Goldstein later shared that mobster and bootlegger Waxie Gordon owned 50% of him, and had been in his corner screaming at him to knock out Hudkins. Gordon had bet Nick the Greek $50,000.00 that "the Ace" would be knocked out.

Goldstein and his wife had a contented later life after he turned referee, and traveled the country making speeches. In 1950, 24 years after the big fight, Ruby was still being asked about Ace Hudkins. He said,

"There is another question they always ask me. They ask about Ace Hudkins. You would think…that this was the only fight I ever had. Why don't they ask me about some of the fights I won? Why don't they ask me about Sid Terries and Jimmy McLarnin? They knocked me out too, but no. It always has to be Ace Hudkins." Ruby kept his sense of humor and whenever he gave a speech at a University, he would start by saying, "If there are any professors of English in the audience, there's still time for them to leave."

Ace had this to say about Ruby Goldstein and that most important fight:

The Arena Oct 10, 1929,

"That Goldstein could fight...believe me, he was the toughest guy I ever fought, and I've battled plenty.

He was a great boxer, with a kick in either mitt and he dropped me for a six-count in the first round. He shed my punches like I wasn't even throwin' my gloves at all, and then he pops he right on the chin and down I go.

But I finally got him. He couldn't hurt me. Nobody can hurt me. I waded right out after him, and he backed up. He kept shooting both hands all the time and he gave me plenty, but I was out to get him and when I finally caught up, I got him...

I caught up with him in the fourth...and I landed a right-hand punch flush on the button. They must have heard that wallop clear up in Boston. But he's got plenty of heart. I'll give him credit for that. He bounced right up and slapped me in the face till my teeth rattled. But I ducked out of the clinch he was reaching for, and sent one from the hip. He went down again-for six, I think- and then he pulled up. That guy had plenty of guts.

There wasn't anything in the world that could have stopped me then. I drove after him, landed another perfect punch right on the button, and he sailed into the ropes, hanging almost upside down, and dead to the world.

They tell me Nick the Greek won $100,000.00 on that fight. I know Goldstein was a 4-1 favorite, but I showed 'em in New York, just as I'd showed 'em in California."

Following his success at Coney Island, Ace was the new "Golden Boy" of boxing, being pursued for endorsements and interviews. They all wanted to know who this Wildcat from Nebraska was.

After the win, Ace and Clyde decided to go home and visit their Mother. They sent the following telegram to The Lincoln Star: *"Will arrive Lincoln Tuesday night via Burlington. Regards to Lincoln friends. Ace and Clyde."*

22 A clipping from Ace Hudkins' Scrapbook. Unknown Portrait/ Illustration by J. (A. or H.) Winters, 1920's.

Extra! Extra!

How to make it in the Big Apple.

"New York likes its own children. Ace Hudkins was adopted only when he proved his mettle by hanging Ruby Goldstein over the ropes like the Tuesday wash."

– News clipping from Ace's scrapbook

"Ace Hudkins is a showman as well as a fighter. The tow-head from Nebraska always leaps and jumps to his corner after every round. He wears a cap turned sideways on his head into the ring— showmanship and nothing less."

Newspaper clipping from Ace's scrapbook

23 An early advertisement for Everlast products, featuring Ace.

In other news: Seabiscuit's jockey, John "Red" Pollard boxed unsuccessfully for a while and used the ring name "Cougar" in tribute to "The Nebraska Wildcat."

On May 14, 1926, Ace spent two days in jail for speeding at 33 mph. The Judge, Municipal Judge Chambers, was waging war on speeding motorists and had sentenced 54 others in three days. Comedian, Ben Turpin, was to be seen by the same judge, on the same charge, the next day.

1927

Lucky Lindy and The Bloodiest Fight Ever Seen

January 10, 1927, Nebraska Memories.

Ace fought one of his return professional matches in the town where he grew up at the University of Nebraska Fieldhouse Coliseum in Lincoln, Nebraska. Ace came back after having beaten Ruby Goldstein and what a way to return to the town where he grew up. The fight was supposed to be held at the City Auditorium, however a fire required moving the match. Governor Adam McMullen, members of the Senate and House of Representatives were scheduled to be there. He must have felt a million emotions as he walked into the Coliseum to fight his buddy Pat Corbett. The Nebraska State Journal describes the match this way:

"Most of the fighting was done in and around Corbett's corner. Ace would come tearing forth with the bell, meeting Pat before the latter had taken over a pace or two from his chair.

The worst sessions Corbett had was in the two closing rounds. He smacked Ace with a straight left to the chin, the best blow he landed, and it stung the Wildcat. He crashed into Pat with a series of blows to the head and body that had Corbett in distress. The west coaster weaved out of the barrage and clung until the bell.

Every round went to Hudkins. Corbett landed frequently but his blows were taps on the wrist compared to the slashing attack of the Wildcat."

Pat Corbett lost in Round 10 but Ace was not done by any means, and he returned to Nebraska twice more. On January 6, 1928, he fought Mike Rozgall at City Auditorium in Omaha, and won. Then there was Buck Holley on June 5, 1928, whom he fought and beat at Landis Field Arena in Lincoln, and this was the first time that he showed the home crowd in person that he had made good.

A Star-Studded Night

February 1, 1927

What a night at The Olympic Auditorium! Ace was set to fight Billy Alger. As he entered he started to hear who was in the crowd. Now, he was used to movie people coming to see him, but he started to hear names like, Jack Gilbert *Monte Cristo, He Who Gets Slapped*, Huntley Gordon, *Stage Door*, and Alan Hale (an actor known for *The Adventures Of Robin Hood,* and *Gentleman Jim*, both of which the Hudkins worked on later for Warner Bros.). The "Man of A Thousand Faces" Lon Chaney was there, as was Dick Barthelmess, of *Dawn Patrol* and *Only Angels Have Wings*, Ray Schrock (uncredited adaptation writer of *The Phantom Of The Opera*), and comedian Harry Langdon of *Hooks and Jabs*. Bert Nelson (wild animal trainer for *Tarzan And His Mate* and *Tarzan, The Ape Man*) gave Ace a real baby wildcat at this event!

    Was Ace intimidated by all of these stars? Not at all – and, he went on to win to prove it! Although Clyde was generally against Ace going into the moving picture business, he was in talks at that time for Ace to make a film showing his boxing prowess.

Extra! Extra! Paul Gallico

Paul Gallico

1897-1976

Paul Gallico was a famous sports-and fiction writer, and sports editor for the New York Daily News. He sparred with Jack Dempsey so that he could describe the feeling of being knocked out by the champ. He wrote the material on which the movies *The Pride Of the Yankees, The Clock, Lili, The Three Lives of Thomasina, The Poseidon Adventure,* and *Mrs. 'Arris Goes To Paris* were based.

Paul Gallico wrote of Ace: "*Untamed Fury...Indeed, he was never a world's champion; but he was tough, hard, mean, cantankerous, combative, fast, courageous, and filled at all times with bitter and flaming lust for battle...He was barred from New York rings simply because he was everything and all that a prizefighter should be.*"

Lincoln Evening Journal, 1955

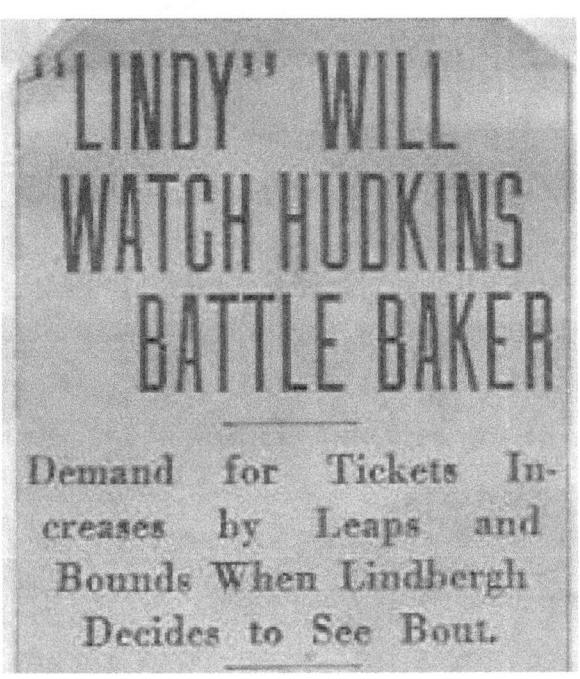

24 Clipping from Ace Hudkins' Scrapbook.

LINDBERGH TO SEE HUDKINS FIGHT SAMMY BAKER TONIGHT

By Special Leased Wire.

New York, June 14.—Boxing fans are in line for an unusual bargain at the Polo grounds Wednesday night when not only will a good program of boxing bouts be presented, but Mayor James Walker is to bring Colonel Charles A. Lindbergh, transatlantic aviator, to the battleground and present him in person from the ring.

Lindbergh had expressed a desire to see his friend, Ace Hudkins, in action against Sergeant Sammy Baker and this bout will be put on immediately after the first preliminary, which gets under way at 8:15, so that the famous airman can see it and get away for the rest of a busy evening elsewhere.

Realizing that Lindy's presence may precipitate a small-sized riot by overzealous fans anxious to get a closeup of the guest of honor, there will be a detail of five hundred policemen on the job to preserve order and to give the international hero safe conduct.

Lindy likely will see his friend from Lincoln, Neb., at his best. Hudkins is facing a formidable foe in Baker but Ace is a favorite to cop. The other bouts which Lindy will not wait around for include Sid Terris against Ruby Goldstein, his east side rival, for six rounds; Billy Petrolle and Billy Wallace in a 10-rounder, and Kid Kaplan and Jackie Fields in another 10.

The show is for the benefit of the Catholic Boys club of New York and the gate is expected to approximate 100 thousand dollars.

25 Ace was excited to have Lindbergh watch him box, and he was favored to win! (Ace Hudkins' Scrapbook Clipping)

June 16, 1927

<u>Lucky Lindy and The Wildcat</u>

"Ace Hudkins, known to the prize ring as the "Nebraska Wildcat," is traveling as steadily and as speedily toward the welterweight championship of the world as Capt. Charles Lindbergh piloted his famous airplane on that now famous nonstop trip from New York to Paris."

Omaha Newspaper June 1927

Flight. Soaring above the clouds. Ever since the Wright brothers first flew in 1903, pilots kept pushing the boundaries and breaking flight records. Charles Lindbergh piloted the first solo transatlantic flight from Long Island, New York to Paris, France on May 20-21, 1927 and was instantly a star. With his blond hair and handsome looks, plus his daring flight, his popularity was as big as any Hollywood star of the time if not bigger. There were songs written for him such as *"Plucky Lindy's Lucky Day,"* by Vernon Dalhart, *"Lucky Lindbergh,"* by Yale Baker's Dozen, and *"When Lindy Comes Home,"* by the Happiness Boys, among many other songs and even a brand-new dance named after him in late May of 1927 called "The Lindy Hop."

In much the same way, records were being made and broken in the boxing world during the

1920's. The Catholic Boys Club hosted a charity carnival and boxing match at The Polo Grounds with guest of honor Charles Lindbergh. At this match, Ace was to box Sammy Baker. According to The Morning Call Newspaper, when Lindbergh heard that Ace would be fighting, he said, *"That's enough for me. If Hudkins is going to box I want to be there...Hudkins is my friend. I knew him in Lincoln when we were both just a couple of kids. Say I'll be mighty glad to see him."* Not only did Lindbergh agree to attend to see Ace, but the promoters re-arranged the order of bouts so that Lindbergh could see Ace fight before Lindy had to leave.

    The boxing world had looked upon Lindbergh, much as the entire country had, with respect and awe. While Lindy was taking off to Paris the entire crowd at the Sharkey-Maloney bout bowed their heads silently in prayer for him. Someone in the crowd shouted, *"Yeah, and that kid's got more guts than any prize fighter alive!"* The fighters concurred. Furthermore, while Lindy had been learning to fly, Ace had been learning to fight in a little gym not far from the flying field in Lincoln. Because of this the demand for tickets to The Catholic Boys Fund bout between Hudkins and Baker went through the roof and police were summoned to protect Lindbergh from the enormous crowd. He only had time to watch one bout, and it was to be Hudkins'.

Ace was eating dinner after training at Madame Bey's Training Camp when, according to 'The Morning Call', he heard the news, and exclaimed, "*Oh boy, ain't it great. Lindbergh is coming to see me fight!*" At that, all present began to celebrate by throwing dishes on the floor to the degree that Ace felt obliged to promise Madame Bey that he would replace her dishes with china.

An Omaha paper from June 1927 read, "*Two young blondes from the middle west will attend charity boxing bouts at the Polo grounds Wednesday night. One is Colonel Charles A. Lindbergh who will look on as the guest of Mayor Walker; the other is Ace Hudkins welterweight sensation, who is billed to battle Sammy Baker.*"

Now, Art wanted Ace to keep training for the upcoming Baker bout and forgo the Catholic Boys Club match but Ace would have none of it. The argument escalated to such a degree that Art finally locked Ace in a bedroom and the Wildcat threatened to leave through the window if his brother didn't let him out! He couldn't stay home and miss this- being mentioned alongside Lindbergh? No way was he staying put! It was a subdued Art and happy Ace that appeared at the Boys Club.

However, Ace may well have wished that Art had kept him locked up that night as the fight resulted in Baker cutting Ace's eye, and with the crowd yelling, "Stop it!'" The referee did so. He stopped the fight in the seventh round, with Ace begging, "Don't stop it. Please don't stop it!" and, "I'm all right. I ain't hurt." The referee thought differently.

Lindbergh arrived late, during the second round. A preliminary bout was fought while the crowd waited for him, and his entrance. During the second round he arrived, with the crowd roaring, and shouting "Hello Slim!", sending flashbulbs popping at his entrance. He looked on with sympathy, as he and Mayor Walker nodded toward Ace as he fought bravely on.

Ace had bought a gift for Charles Lindbergh, but was not able to present it personally the way that he would have wanted, due to the fact that he was recovering after the fight. The gift was presented from inside the ring by Joe Humphries. It was a heart-shaped box lined with purple silk and inside were a pair of golden boxing gloves with the inscription: *From the Ace of the ring to the ace of the air.* Lindbergh thanked Ace via Humphries, then expressed further thankfulness for the prayers that had come from many of the same fight fans on the night of his flight.

Unfortunately, the Catholic Boys Club lost money that night, causing some to cry foul. Ace stepped up and donated $700.00 of his earnings for that evening, as did other fighters. After the fight, sportswriter Frederick Ware questioned, in his *The Sportolog* column, whether Ace had been intimidated by having the great aviation hero in the audience. He may have had a point -it is difficult to over-emphasize the popularity of "Lucky Lindy." Ace was well known for being extremely confident, but that confidence was not evident this night. It is entirely possible he had been overwhelmed by the larger-than-life reputation of Lindbergh and the unadulterated love that the crowd had for him. The cheers that rose on that night had been for Lindbergh and not for the boxers. Could he have been psyched out? After all, sometimes victories are won mentally as well as physically.

    Ace's brother Clyde was unable to be there on that night, and it was rumored that this also may have had an adverse effect on the Ace. We may never know exactly what went wrong for him.

<u>Extra! Extra!</u>

<u>Ace and the Aviators</u>

26 Ace and Art with unknown aviators. (Author's Collection)

"A few years ago when Lindbergh was taking flying lessons at an aviation school in Lincoln, Neb., Hudkins was just breaking in as a preliminary boxer. The three Hudkins brothers- Ace, Deuce and Trey- lived just two blocks distant from Lindbergh. The embryo flier became a fast friend of the embryo boxer. Now Lindbergh is champion of the air and Hudkins is not far from being a champion of the ring. Ace has lived up to his name. All the Hudkins brothers ran true to form. Ace is a high card, Deuce and Trey the older brothers, have been tossed into the fistic discard."

The Morning Call June 15, 1927

27 Art with an unknown aviator.

Extra! Extra! The Funnies!

Cauliflower Alley Notes, July 1927:

Ab. Hudkins, known as the Sherlock Holmes of the Hudkins training camp, has a German police dog on which he tried to swing the name of Rin Tin Tin II. Finding he couldn't pull it off, he hit upon Gin Gin Gin as a happy substitute. Every time Ab. calls his pet about a dozen bootleggers bob up from neighboring bushes. Several days ago a friend of Ab's ventured: "He's a dandy bloodhound." "No, no," objected Hudkins, "he's a dandy gin hound."

Extra! Extra!

Madame Bey's Training Camp

Ace bragged so much about the eats that brother Art fell for the camp life and shifted his abode from New York. The first crack out of the box Art ordered a broiled spring chicken. "What is that?" smiled Art as he raised one of the hard-hearted legs from his plate and waved it at the madame. "That is one of my tenderest Rhode Islands," came the meek reply. "I haven't anything against the State of Rhode Island," whimpered Ace's brother, 'but I want to tell you right now that this same leg must have been doing road work ever since Berlenbach was back in Los Angeles and that's some eight years ago." Thus chivalry ends at the china closet.

Los Angeles Paper – July 1927

<u>Extra! Extra!</u>
<u>Preparing For Another Round With Sammy.</u>

One of many clippings from Ace Hudkins' scrapbooks states,

> *"Wild As Ever—Ace Hudkins, the "Nebraska Wildcat", is ready for his bout with Seargent Sammy Baker at Wrigley Field on July 25.*
>
> *Hudkins bears no outward ill effects of his battle with Baker in New York a month ago when the Mitchell Field soldier surprised the boxing world by stopping Ace in seven rounds. Ace carries a slight scar over his right eye-lid which is only visible when the eye is closed. Yes sir, he's the same old wildcat – only wilder than ever."*

"Ace Hudkins is as "cocky" as ever. A defeat at the hands of Baker in New York did not alter the "Nebraska Wildcat's" confidence in himself. This picture is the most typical ever taken of him. It shows him puffing out his chest in self-satisfaction *just like Ace does when he thinks of how good he is." "I'll knock Baker out in the sixth or seventh round." Ace Hudkins*

"But in spite of Baker's impressive record there is confidence galore in the Hudkins camp. Ace has worked harder for this fight than any other in his life. He is really 'rarin' to go, and when he is unleashed against his New York conqueror the cash customers can bank on plenty of action. It won't be a tea party."

Los Angeles Paper- July 1927

"A number of local wiseacres look to see Baker knock out Ace inside of seven rounds. Now lads, just bear down on the old purse strings and visit Wrigley Feld tomorrow night. If you don't see one of the greatest slugging bouts of all times, then judgement has fled to brutish beasts and men have lost their reason."

Los Angeles Paper- July 1927

Nebraska "Wildcat" Becomes Pet

"Ace Hudkins, well known wild cat among the welters, has become the pet of Broadway fight fans and all New York. Ace stopped off several months ago, and was the cause of no little excitement, many long faces and lean purses by stopping Ruby Goldstein. The cat came back recently and wailed the whey out of Al Mello at the Queensboro club. He did the job in such an artistic manner and showed such rare ability as a fighter that the N.Y. Commission has declared him the leading contender for the welterweight title. I have been informed on very good authority that the Iron Man of fistiana, the venerable Wm. Muldoon, has expressed the opinion that Ace Hudkins is the best welterweight in the world."

Self Defense, July 1927

July 25, 1927

Sergeant Sammy Baker Versus Ace "Nebraska Wildcat" Hudkins:
The Bloodiest Fight Ever Seen

On June 15, 1927 Sergeant Sammy Baker won, by a TKO, his fight against Ace. It took 7 rounds at the Polo Grounds in New York, with none other than Charles Lindbergh in the audience to witness the brawl. It was the only time Ace had a Technical Knock Out, meaning that the referee judged him as unable to continue.

He was not knocked out- but, he had lost the match, and 40,000 people saw it. Never one to take losing well, "The Wildcat" wanted another shot. On July 25, at Wrigley Field in Los Angeles, he got his chance.

Despite a technical knockout in the previous match, California fans were still behind Ace. *"The fact that Hudkins' followers have forced the earlier odds on Baker to even money is a remarkable tribute to the California popularity of the Nebraska fistic product."* claimed an Omaha paper in July 1927. In fact, fans were so thrilled to see this bout that when the ticket office opened at Wrigley Field at 2 o'clock there was already a line in the mid-day heat, and when bleacher seats were put on sale at 3 o'clock there was a positive rush to get a ticket. Scalpers were selling their tickets for double the legitimate asking price and the fight grossed $91,000.00 in tickets.

This would turn out to be the bloodiest battle the ring had seen up to this point and it lasted ten rounds. In the fourth, Baker went down for a count of 9 and in the fifth, Ace broke his hand. In the ninth round, Ace was down for a count of 1 but, in the tenth round, Ace was awarded the win. Said Baker as the fight was ended, "I lost, but I did my best."

28 Sammy Baker fight crowd! Just a portion of the 40,000 spectators who came to see the Baker-Hudkins fight! Keystone Photo Service Los Angeles paper 1927. (Ace Hudkins Scrapbook Clipping)

Ace Hudkins put it all over Sammy Baker in their 12-round go at Madison Square Garden in New York. This makes Ace the leading contender for a match with Joe Dundee.

29 Ace Letting Baker Have it! & Sammy Baker (Ace Hudkins' Scrapbook Clippings)

30 A battle for blood was the spectacular bout between Sammy Baker and Ace Hudkins. (Ace Hudkins' Scrapbook Clipping)

31 Baker almost out! (Ace Hudkins' Scrapbook Clipping)

Grantland Rice, the great poet and sportswriter describes the professional differences between Sammy Baker and Ace in this way:

"Take the case of Sergeant Sammy Baker...and his archenemy Ace Hudkins. When they met some while back in New York, Baker seemed to be a trifle the better boxer, just as hard a hitter, just as fast and just about as courageous.

But printed in large letters on the back of Hudkins' fighting toga was WILDCAT and the Nebraskan seemed to be well acquainted with that animal's mode of warfare. He had no idea of permitting Baker to use his boxing skill and his sloughing ability.

He simply piled in on top of Baker with both hands working at top speed, hammering and thumping, jabbing and jolting, until Baker suddenly found himself on the defensive with all his time taken up with self-protection.

The Wild Cat's rush had thrown him off balance mentally and physically. And so strong was the flame in Hudkins' soul that he refused to do any slowing down-even when Baker nailed him on the point of the chin with a full-swinging right hand. The Nebraskan's knees sagged, his head snapped back, his body quivered, but he kept on surging in with both fists flying."

Feb 17, 1928 "The Wildcat" and "The Sergeant" had their final re-match in New York where Hudkins again won in 10.

Extra! Extra!
                Robert L. Ripley

Found in Ace's scrapbook is a caricature and article by the great Robert L. Ripley (1890-1949), of Ripley's Believe It or Not. He was known as an explorer, columnists, and curator of interesting facts from around the world.

In this article, Ripley claims, *"There has never been a fighter more aptly named than Ace 'Wildcat' Hudkins. He fights with the feline ferocity if ever a human did. And he never stops…strength, endurance, and everlasting aggressiveness. Ace has a great chance to win the welterweight title. He will soon meet the new champion, Joe Dundee, and when he does the fur will fly, for he is a sure-enough wildcat."*

**32 Can't Hit Ace Now, Los Angeles Referee Aug 1927
(Ace Hudkins' Scrapbook Clipping)**

Can't Hit Ace Now!

Ace Hudkins will celebrate his twenty-second birthday this month. On August 30 the Hudkins family will get together and have a big party at Ace's home on Los Feliz Boulevard.

Hudkins is after Joe Dundee and his welterweight title, but for a fight with a fighter like Dundee Ace wants his share of the gate receipts.

Max Waxman, Dundee's manager, is after a guarantee of $100,000 for the match, which leaves little for Hudkins or the promoter who stages the bout.

Hudkins put on the ball player's catcher's mask last week in the gymnasium and offered to let any boxer in the gym take a "Mary Anne" at his chin.

"You're tough enough, Ace, you don't need a mask," came the reply from the fighters gathered around. –Ace Hudkins' scrapbook clipping.

Extra! Extra!

On the Road with Ace

As Ace traveled across America, he made many stops and met many great people. Everywhere Ace went, crowds were sure to follow. Everyone, from governors to local fight fans, wanted to meet the Wildcat. Mayor Hess of Las Vegas was just one of the multitude of fans Ace had. If only we could have hopped a ride on the rails along with him.

Extra! Extra!

Changing Weight Classes

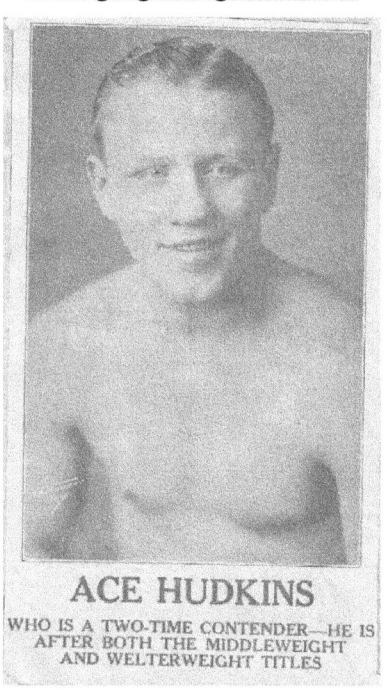

33 Ace wanted it all—Middleweight and Heavyweight titles! (Ace Hudkins' Scrapbook Clipping)

Thomas Hearns, Sugar Ray Leonard, Oscar De La Hoya: These are some of the names of those who have fought in different weight classes and we can add Ace "The Wildcat" Hudkins to that list. He fought in weight classes from Lightweight to Middleweight, to Welterweight, to light Heavyweight- an impressive feat, and he seemed to succeed best in the lighter weights. Nephew, Rich Brehm stated, *"Ace started out as a featherweight, and I guess he ended up as a heavyweight."* Unfortunately, he did less well as he gained in weight. He was a natural in Middleweight.

34 A cartoon about Ace leaving behind the Lightweight and Welterweight divisions to pursue the Middleweight title. Unknown artist. (Ace Hudkins' Scrapbook Clipping)

Ace was a popular subject of comic strips in the 1920's and here are examples depicting him gaining weight as he prepares to box Sammy Baker and as he moved from lightweight to welterweight to middleweight. In order to fight for the Middleweight Championship of the World against Mickey Walker, Ace had to gain weight to move up in class.

35 & 36 Cartoons about Ace moving from Middleweight to Light Heavyweight, and Sammy Baker laughing at him.

<u>Extra! Extra!</u>

<u>Working out with Ace!</u>

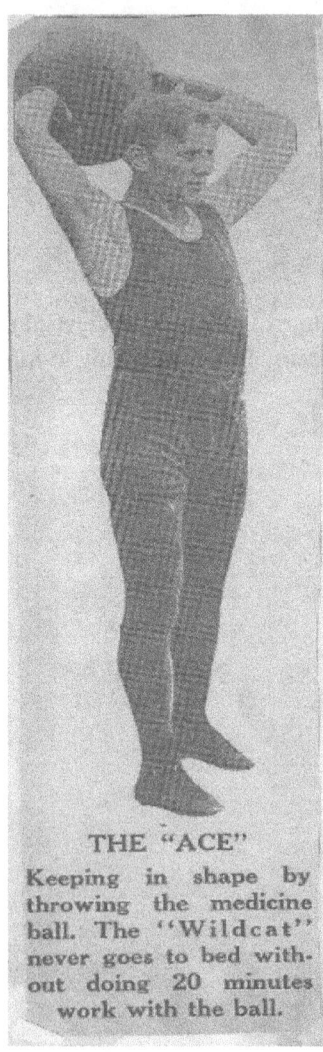

37 Ace working with the medicine ball. (Ace Hudkins' Scrapbook Clipping)

38 Art, Fon, Ace and friends. (Ace Hudkins' Scrapbook Clipping)

" ...Joe Benjamin, ...Mushy Callahan...Ruby Goldstein...One fighter is responsible for the downfall of these good men. His name is Ace Hudkins...Hudkins has sent more men from the front ranks of contenders than any fighter in the game to-day... He is what people of erudition like Mr. Tunney would call a "wow." In the tall sticks they call him a "ding buster," by heck...He thrills them and sends them home satisfied. To the spectator he is a darling; to the poor, harried promoter he is a sure box office attraction and to his opponents he is nobody's business."

Self Defense, July 1927

Ace Hudkins Puts Them Through

Extra! Extra! Ace Stories

Dick, That's How He Got The Packard

Dick Donald has suspended the free list to the Ace Hudkins-Sammy Baker debacle Monday night at Wrigley Field.

"*It isn't the boys who can't pay that mooch the passes,*" said Donald. "*It's the fellows who have the dough and won't part with it that I want to cut off the list.*"

Donald tells a little yarn about being followed for three days by one unusually persistent acquaintance who wanted a "comp" for the Colima-Hudkins bout.

Two days following the show Donald saw the fellow on the Speedway at Venice. The pass "moocher" was driving a Packard sedan.

-Ace Hudkins Scrapbook clipping

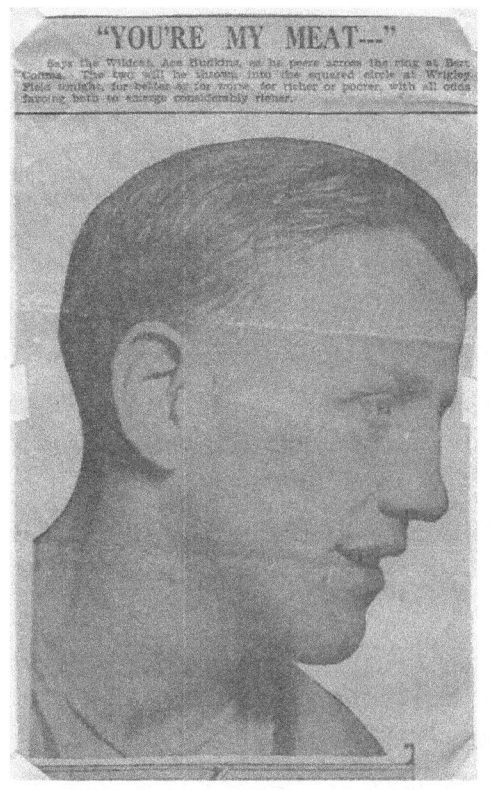

39   You're My Meat! (Ace Hudkins' Scrapbook Clipping)

""You're My Meat---" says the Wildcat Ace Hudkins, as he peers across the ring at Bert Colima. The two will be thrown into the squared circle at Wrigley Field tonight, for better or for worse, for richer or poorer, with all odds favoring both to emerge considerably richer."

(Ace Hudkins' Scrapbook Clipping)

"Is he sardonic or leering? Bert Colima will give you the answer tomorrow night at Wrigley field, for he will study the face above more closely than any other individual when he swaps punches with its owner, Mr. Ace Hudkins, a wildcat from Nebraska."

(Ace Hudkins' Scrapbook Clipping.)

April 1927: *"Ace gained a suspension in Kansas because he had scheduled to fight a former sparring partner Sid Socklyn but- Sid had signed to fight Ace under a fake name. When authorities found out, both men were censured. In order to fight Sammy Baker, Ace wanted to clear his name in Kansas, which would clear his name in New York as well. The California Commissioner said: "Californians think well of Ace as a fighter and a good kid. He has never done a thing to cause the commissioners any worry. Some fight experts think he is a rough and foul fighter but that sentiment comes mostly from the sympathizers of Hudkins's (sic) opponents. Ace is a hard fellow on opponents when he thinks he has to be, but as a rule he usually keeps from unmercifully punishing an opponent when he has the fight won." "*

Los Angeles Paper, April 1927, Hudkins' Scrapbook Clipping

Why Censure Hudkins and His Partner?
By Westbrook Pegler by special leased wire

New York, March 28- A few weeks ago there was an indignant outcry by some mid-western prizefight commission because Ace Hudkins, one of their own, had tried to ring in one of his sparring partners as an opponent in a bout. The mid-westerners must have become very touchy, because when Joe Lynch was champion, he and a young friend from New York fought 17 bouts in 17 towns, and the other young man never used the same name twice. However, they did put up a good fight and the other young man had a rare gift to color the combat. He was what the boys call an easy bleeder and when he would finally go down under terrific volleys of lefts and rights to the shoulder and neck, his face would be painted with gore from a bruised ear. "It made the fight very interesting and realistic," one of Mr. Lynch's managers explained in later years. "This boy could almost turn that ear on and off like a spigot in a keg. An ear like that is worth a lot of money to a club fighter". Hudkins' Scrapbook Clipping

Many sports journalists who saw Ace as a beginner thought him to be a scrawny hayseed. Ace himself mentioned that, when he first arrived in Hollywood, he didn't know how he would fight as he hadn't been eating regularly. Soon enough though, those jounalists saw the wild in the Wildcat, and began to eat their words. Here is what one journalist admitted in a clipping from the Hudkins Scrapbook:

> *"On occasions as this evening when Ace Hudkins attempts to out-thump somebody or other (in this case Lew Tendler,) we are always reminded of the occasion when we wandered out to the Hollywood Stadium one Friday morning and Cap Strelinger invited us in to see them weigh the principals for the main event that evening, towit, Tommy Carter, existing Coast lightweight champion, and a scrawny, flat-chested, washed-out-looking blond youngster, said to be a newsboy from Nebraska. We felt like telling the kid he ought to take up some other means of earning his oats and felt quite sure that if the well-muscled Carter socked the kid on that chest, his fist would go clear through and come out the other side. Well, we picked up the paper the next morning to learn that he deprived Mr. Carter of his title, and we never did believe it was the same kid we saw until some time*

later when we watched him plaster Joe Benjamin to a fare-thee-well out at Vernon. Moral, don't bet on our judgement of fighters."

(Ace Hudkins' Scrapbook Clipping)

As soon as Ace was temporarily suspended, journalists, as is their wont, came out of the woodwork with smart remarks and tried to make a buck. One reporter wrote this dismissive account of Ace's situation, which comes from Ace's own scrapbook. The woman's case was later dismissed.:

"Hudkins, lightweight boxer, Lincoln, Neb. is the way he is listed in "Dem's Dose." He was named after a playing card, and right now is called an "Ace in the Hole." For Mr. Hudkins' name is also mud on all states including the Scandinavian, and excluding Pennsylvania and California. Boxing commissions in many places have scratched him from their list of "starters" because of recent events that did not smell, mighty lak' a rose.

Nevertheless "Ace" is from Nebraska and has numbed the brain of many an aspiring boxer, to say nothing of being a sudden cure for insomnia.

Oh, Yes, The Rasslers

Men who keep up on such matters say, "Ace is not ripe." Others say he is "more than mellow," but none of them wants to fight him. It was in the bleak of November that "Ace" began his raven [The meaning of "raven" in this context is not clear. It may mean, "to rave."]. *At this time a young lady accused him of slapping her face. Should Ace have been tried by court martial, he would probably have been burned at the stake, but being a very mere civilian, he was fined $1 and costs. He appealed and later the case was dismissed."*

(Ace Hudkins' Scrapbook Clipping)

Extra! Extra!

Ace's Victories and Fun Facts!

40 Cartoon displaying some of Ace's victories. Possibly from an Olympic Auditorium program. (Ace Hudkins' Scrapbook Clipping)

"Ace Hudkins is the most sensational fighter in the whole wide world." Frank Kerwin

"I want none of Ace Hudkins for Mickey Walker, Hudkins is too rough and tough." Jack Kearns

A popularity contest run by *The Los Angeles Referee* in June 1927 saw Ace Hudkins fans send in 16,500 coupons and subscriptions to send him to the top, at least temporarily, as the Most Popular Boxer!

While fighting Colima, Ace appeared in a, *"nice new blue and white bathrobe with the likeness of a wildcat stamped on the back of it."*

41 Clipping written by Damon Runyon. (Ace Hudkins' Scrapbook Clipping)

Even Damon Runyon had to admit upon seeing Ace that "...*fighting a den of wildcats could not be much more strenuous than facing the ripping, tearing, flailing Hudkins in a roped arena.*" (See above)

42 Advertisement for an opening of a club where both Sammy Baker and Ace were to be honored. (Ace Hudkins' Scrapbook Clipping)

Ace Fights Tendler, and The IRS Wants It's Share

There was such a crowd before the Tendler bout that police were unable to control it, and several women fainted. This left the scalpers to sell $50.00 ringside tickets, which still did not deter demand!

The fight broke records for California indoor fights with receipts grossing $32,855.

Immediately the IRS claimed that Hudkins owed $447.17 for 1924, and $12,367.77 for 1926, so they held his purse until payment arrangements were made. Ace's estimated income for 1925-1926 was approximately $100,000.00. Ace posted a $19,000.00 bond and the lien was lifted.

43 Cartoon of Ace and Lew Tendler. (Ace Hudkins' Scrapbook Clipping)

Ace and Lew would do anything to get the fans off their seats!

Extra! Extra!
Could Ace Have Earned a Double Title?

Making order out of chaos: Making an argument for Ace being capable of both a Welterweight and Middleweight Championship.

Roberts knocked out Dundee (Welterweight Champ)
Mello knocked out Roberts
Ace knocked out Mello

Therefore: Ace could knock out Dundee the Champ.

Lomski beat Flowers (Middleweight Champ)
Anderson beat Lomski
Colima beat Anderson
Ace beat Colima

Therefore: Ace could beat the Middleweight Champ.

It appears that Ace could have gone all the way with both titles, had conditions been right!

"I SHOULD WORRY," SAYS ACE

The "Wildcat" had a warm-up fight last week, knocking out Arizona Joe Rivers at Phoenix. Hudkins meets Joe Dundee, the welterweight champion, at Wrigley Field next month.

If he loses to Dundee Ace will quit the ring and smoke cigars and count his money the rest of his life. The "Wildcat" shown above, wearing high plugged lid, likes his cigars. He smokes plenty plenty of them but never inhales the smoke.

44 I should worry! Los Angeles Referee, OCT. 1927 (Ace Hudkins' Scrapbook Clipping)

"If he loses to Dundee, Ace will quit the ring and smoke cigars and count his money the rest of his life. The "Wildcat," wearing high plugged lid, likes his cigars. He smokes plenty of them but never inhales the smoke."

Extra! Extra!

Ace's Gentle Ways!

"He is mild-mannered out of the ring, friendly with everybody, talking to youngsters, whistling to and making friends with stray dogs, careful with his money. In the ring he is a changed man. He fights from the first gong to the last. He never lets up a minute. He's the Dempsey style of killer. That's why he's the "Nebraska Wildcat.""

45 Ace, approximately 1938 with nephews Clyde and Gene Sader. (Author's Collection)

46 Ace, Clyde and Art answering fan mail while they wait in great anticipation to fight Joe Dundee!

Extra! Extra!
Clyde and The Movies

At Home In Los Angeles, California

FILMS AND STAGE DO A FIGHTER NO GOOD

CLYDE HUDKINS, MANAGER OF THE NEBRASKA WILDCAT, SAYS IT RUINS A GOOD FIGHTER

Clyde Hudkins

It is interesting to note that Clyde was a vocal opponent of Ace entering the entertainment field. In an article in the October 1927 edition of *The Los Angeles Referee*, Clyde says the following:

"I have made a study of fighters who have gone on the stage and who have fallen for the films and I have come to the conclusion that such a life will rob and take all the best that a good fighter has to offer- it absolutely robs him of his stamina and when a fighter loses this he is done.

"Night life- eating at all hours- filling the stomach up with the rich foods of night life will sap the powers of any fighter and I have steered clear of such a life for the 'Wildcat,' and as long as he is under my management, I will not permit of him entering the movies and making tours on the stage, although I have had offers for him several times. I do not claim that a few weeks will do any material damage but any kind of a siege along those lines will make a great fighter just an ordinary one."

He then goes on to talk about the negative results that have befallen other boxers who took to the stage in Vaudeville or appeared in films:

"Dempsey lost a lot of his stuff while in the films. Why, go back to Sullivan- the travelling around with shows ruined him-- he had a strong constitution and it took some time to do it, but nevertheless it did it in the end. Sullivan would have

reigned many years longer had he kept away from the stage and touring life."

"Corbett fell for the stage- had it not been for his stage life, I am willing to come out flat-footed and say that he would probably have regained his title when he fought Jeff.."

"Fitzsimmons ruined himself by the stage work. Willard was with a circus and went to pieces. The stage work that Jeffries did, ruined him."

There was one exception, according to Clyde:

"Tunney seems to be different from them all- looks like he might do a lot of stage and film work and never be effected, as he avoids all the things that ruined the other men. He will not eat at night- he keeps the best of hours. While it will slow him up physically he avoids the thing that ruins one."

Clyde then explained the offers he has had for Ace, and he left the door slightly ajar:

"I have had offers for Ace to do stage work- right now I have a letter from one of the biggest vaudeville circuits- offering a contract for Ace over their circuit if he wins Dundee. I have turned it down. If the contract was short and the money long- I might consider it, otherwise absolutely not."

Ready To Face Dundee

Extra! Extra!

Pre-fight Preparations for Ace Hudkins and Joe Dundee!

While training for the bout, Dundee employed two bodyguards. Manager Waxman claimed that there was a blackmail threat asking for $10,000.00 not to kill Dundee. Police felt the note was a hoax.

Jack Dempsey and Mushy Callahan both watched Dundee in training for this fight. Former boxer -turned- actor The Texas Kid watched both men train at Manhattan Gym. He was known for the movies, *On Thin Ice* (1925), and *One-Round Hogan* (1927).

Ace trained by mountain climbing, horseback riding, and runs in Saugus, CA.

Seeing this tactic, Dundee started training outdoors also.

Both Ace and Dundee also trained at Jack Dempsey's Manhattan Gymnasium, located in Los Angeles.

The fight was postponed from Oct 29 to Nov 3, to Nov 10, and this turned out to be a blessing as Babe Ruth and Lou Gehrig were playing an exhibition game on the 29th in Fresno following the World Series. This undoubtedly would have drawn many people away from the fight.

47 Clipping from The Hudkins Scrapbook.

48 Ace excitedly preparing for Dundee. (Hudkins' Scrapbook

Clipping)

And don't think Ace isn't a showman. He is, every minute of the time. When he's socking he has cocked away in that tousled honey-colored head of his a mental picture of Ace Hudkins. He likes to see them grin at ringside. He loves the spotlight, and with it all, he's a fighter at heart. Every fighter is something of a showman, and Ace excels at both.

Los Angeles Paper, Oct. 1927

"I think I'm a sure thing."

Ace Hudkins, when told that he was a slight favorite over Dundee.

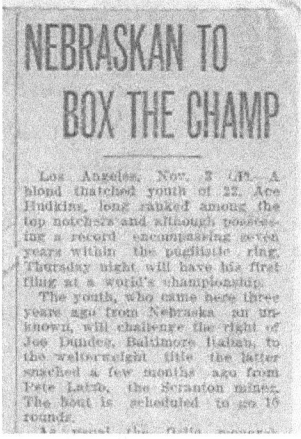

49 The fight would be on the radio!

50 Ready to box the champ. (Hudkins' Scrapbook Clipping)

In the article, "*Ace Hudkins Puts Them Through,*" in the July 1927 edition of *Self Defense,* (page 10), pseudonymous author, Ringster, extrapolates on the attraction that Ace held for fans, and the fear he elicited from fellow fighters:

"...Joe Benjamin,...Mushy Callahan...Ruby Goldstein, ...Burt Colima...

Look these names over carefully...One fighter is responsible for the downfall of these good men. His name is Ace Hudkins...Hudkins has sent more men from the front ranks of contenders than any fighter in the game today. No constitution is proof against his vicious, body punching attack. One by one they met hm and one by one they fell by the wayside...A few, supermen of the ring, withstood his terrific onslaught, but they are few and far between.

What a fightin' fool this dynamic young Mr. Hudkins is. He is what people of erudition like Mr. Tunney would call a "wow." In the tall sticks they call him a "ding buster," by heck. But, whether he is spoken of in words of many syllables or mouthed in the argot of the slums the fact remains that his style of fighting is what the doctor ordered and the cash customers crave. He thrills them and sends them away satisfied. To the spectators he is a darling; to the poor, harried promoter he is a sure box office attraction and to his opponents he is nobody's business.

The ring has not yet seen Ace Hudkins give the best of his ability. It is only in the last few months that he has grown into a welterweight. With youth, a constitution of iron, a heart of fire that dismisses knockdowns with a grin, he is stepping confidently with unreluctant feet to where the contender and the champion meet. This young Nebraskan is due to make ring history that the fisticuff artists will shoot at for years to come. ...

Somewhere in Baltimore, Joe Dundee, the new welterweight champion, hugs his title closely to him and peers anxiously over his shoulder at the shadow of a wildcat on his trail. When these two men meet- the champion a cool, calculating boxer, the contender a rushing, slugging, ripping, clawing, body hammering fighter- Ace Hudkins will be in there fighting his heart out to win the title...

...Ace Hudkins says that he can beat or stop any welterweight in

the world and he says it with an earnestness that detracts nothing from his opponent's ability and makes the statement all the more convincing."

51 Ace deciding which face to wear when he fights Dundee at Halloween time. (Ace Hudkins' Scrapbook Clipping)

52 Ace posing for the camera! 1927. UCLA Library Archives

53 Ace "Putting up his dukes!" 1927. UCLA Library Archives

November 10, 1927

Joe Dundee versus Ace Hudkins:
The Fight That Never Was

Imagine preparing for a fight, the training, the expense, the emotional and mental preparations. Not just any fight, but a world championship! You arrive at the gym. You get dressed. You are a coiled spring, or, more accurately a wildcat ready to pounce on your opponent. Then you wait… and you wait…

Five months before, in June of 1927, with Ace fresh from beating Al Mello, Clyde tried to set up a match with Dundee. Brooklyn promoter, Humbert Fugazy wanted the match badly as he had just lost money on a Dundee-Lazlo fight, and he knew that a Dundee-Hudkins match was just the ticket to recoup his losses. However, Dundee had begged off a previous match with Hudkins claiming an injured ankle, and at this point was mainly interested in fighting Mickey Walker. Dundee would not be required to defend his title for 6 months.

Finally, in November of 1927, the fight was set. This was what Ace had been waiting for, training for- finally, a shot at the title. The World Welterweight Championship! Dundee had won the title in June of 1927, and ever since then Ace had talked of little else than getting that title for himself, going as far as to say that if he lost to Dundee he would hang up his gloves, and if he won, he would defend the title for one bout, then retire! (One can speculate as to whether he was already looking ahead to the movie business, as he had surely received a taste of the perks of movie stardom while sparring with Valentino.) We do know that he claimed he was going to buy a billiard and pool room in Los Angeles.

There was much conjecture and hype concerning a Dundee-Hudkins match, and much hype concerning Ace's previous match with Sammy Baker, "The Bloodiest Fight Ever Seen."

On November 5, the headlines screamed "Dundee Faces Prosecution For Failure To Fight Ace Hudkins" and in giant ¾ inch, or 50-point font DUNDEE REFUSES TO FIGHT; HUDKINS CLAIMS TITLE and HUDKINS FIGHT OFF; ACE CLAIMS TITLE.

What happened? After two mediocre preliminary bouts, in front of an anxious crowd, a horseshoe floral arrangement was brought in to the ring for Dundee. Ace entered the ring in his blue and gray-striped robe and waited. And waited. And waited until nine minutes had passed. Ace recalled, "I strolled into the ring, looked over to the other corner and no one was there." Where was Dundee? Apparently, promoter Dick Donald could not produce the $60,000.00, in cash-not check- that had been his guarantee for fighting Ace. Instead he offered Dundee $23,000.00, and frantically scrambled to come up with the balance just to get Dundee in the ring! He had given Waxman a check for 13,000 additional dollars, but the account was attached by creditors when he attempted

to cash it. This $60,000.00 guarantee was not recognized by the commission, as it was not technically legal. The commission only recognized the percentage agreement that was made on both sides so they ruled that Waxman and Dundee had violated their contract. Dick Donald claimed that if Waxman had let Dundee fight there would have been enough to pay a large portion of the $60,000.00.

Meanwhile, after nine minutes of waiting in the ring for Dundee, Ace left, then reappeared in street clothes while a band played, trying to calm the crowd. At last, they played, *"Home Sweet Home"* as Ace left.

As Ace recalled, *"Finally, the announcer told the audience that the fight was being called off and then all h*** broke loose."* The crowd was furious. Riot is not too strong a word for what occurred: chairs were thrown, fights broke out and police were called.

Tom Kennedy, a former fighter and film comedian of the time, who would become known for *Tillie's Punctured Romance* with W.C. Fields, and *Boston Blackie* movies, amongst many other credits, tried to calm the crowd and stood in the ring to make an announcement. He removed his cap and said, on behalf of Ace, that Hudkins had trained diligently for 6 weeks, and was ready to fight. Dundee had not entered the park, and did not intend to, and that Ace was claiming the World's Welterweight title. If this was meant to calm the crowd, it did not. Although people initially cheered, they then turned their attention to wanting their money back. $10.00 a seat was a large sum in 1927.

As a side note, Ace and Kennedy remained friends and worked together later. Kennedy appeared on the television shows *Maverick* and *Cheyenne*, while Ace provided the horses and wagons for these and other Western shows.

Police riot calls were made and every available officer in the city was sent to Wrigley: 250 officers plus reserves went in. Police battled with the crowd as hundreds climbed into the ring. Chairs were thrown, and nightsticks used. As a portion of the ring collapsed, many tumbled into the press section, damaging typewriters, telegraph instruments, and cameras. Whiskey bottles were hurled, and women fainted as three policemen were removed for medical treatment.

"Two people were killed in the rioting and it marked the first time in the history of professional boxing that a fighter failed to show up for a championship bout."

As the crowd slowly dispersed, thousands grabbed wooden chairs, and outside of the field they started a bonfire. As the firemen and police worked, several thousand tried to crash the box office, only finally being deterred by nightsticks and water. Amazingly, only one arrest was made: of a man who had broken a chair over a policeman's head.

At Dundee's hotel, the Biltmore, more than 100 people created a scene trying to get to him. They were dispersed, but four officers were assigned for his safety. It transpired that if Max Waxman, Dundee's manager, had just let Dundee fight, the house ticket sales, etc. would have more than covered his client's fee.

54 Could Ace claim the title without a fight taking place? (Ace Hudkins' Scrapbook Clipping)

Police looked for them at the Biltmore Hotel, where they had stayed in seclusion since the time of the scheduled match. Joe Dundee and his manager were not there, so the detectives followed the rest of Dundee's group as they went to the Santa Fe Station and boarded the "Chief" headed for Chicago. The detectives then followed a hunch and went to the Pasadena Station, where they found Waxman and Dundee on the train in car 206. Waxman claimed he thought the newspaper reports about warrants being out on them both for false advertising were "just kidding." They were arrested and finger-printed. The charge was false advertising, the clam being that Donald, Waxman, and by association Dundee, continued to sell tickets to a match that they knew could not take place, due to lack of funds. It is possible, as was asserted by Waxman, that Commissioner Strelinger told them, "Why, they haven't got anything on you. You haven't done anything. If you want to go back to Chicago, why go on and beat it." It appears there was a $60,000.00 guarantee for the fight. The gate, or earning for that night's tickets, would have exceeded $80,000. Ace claimed the crown by default, but it was not to be--the boxing commission denied him, calling the fight a "no contest." The ticket holders were ready to file a joint suit against the State Athletic Commission and Dick Donald, however because many ticket holders lost their tickets, and many others were general admission, with no ticket, the crowd did not get its money back. Those who did retain tickets were told they could use them for a future fight, and $20,000.00 went to the Community Chest charity.

Governor C.C. Young was appalled that this could happen in his state. Boxing had a negative reputation in part because in the 1920's it could be a shady business. When he heard about this incident, he "pointed out that the future welfare of the fistic game in the state hinged upon the supervision the commission gave boxing."

There are at least three theories as to why Dundee did not show:

1.) Promoter Dick Donald did not come up with the $60,000 that manager Waxman expected for his client to fight. (The Boxing Commission initially stated that they knew of no other contract than the standard that Dundee was to receive 37 ½ % of the gate, and Hudkins 12 ½ %.)

2.) Waxman wanted a different referee, one of his choosing. Clyde said that, "Dundee wants to insist on Pop O'Brien of Philadelphia as referee. I will not allow this, because George Blake was appointed referee. It is not a question of the money with Dundee at all; he is afraid to box Hudkins on the up and up, without a hand-picked referee. The question was solved; that was just Waxman's excuse to get out of the fight." But Waxman asserted that he had agreed upon Blake, and the commission had added two different referees.

George Blake was a well-liked and respected referee and appeared in the movie *Kid Galahad (1937)* as a referee.

55 George Blake, from Los Angeles Referee, Nov. 1927 (Ace Hudkins' Scrapbook Clipping)

3.) After repeatedly hearing the hype about "The Wildcat," was Dundee afraid? Ace was known to have a certain demeanor in the ring. As George Baker observed, the image of Ace's scowling face *"...was to become the most dreaded sight seen by many a lightweight, welterweight and middleweight of the Hudkins era. It was the face of a killer, a savage who, while in the ring, had nothing in common with his fellow man save a similarity of form. It was a face that, years afterward in the lives of many an ex-pug, came out of the mist of memory and dream to haunt them in their unguarded moments."*

Donald said that the bout could have gone through but for an "*…eleventh hour hunch on the part of Max Waxman and Dundee that the champion could lose his title.*" After all, Ace had beaten Ruby Goldstein-- Ace had left Ruby Goldstein hanging onto the ropes in a half-conscious daze. Ace had also fought the "bloodiest fight ever seen" against Sammy Baker just four months before he and Dundee were to battle. It would, therefore, appear likely that Dundee was concerned that the upstart would beat him, and his championship would be relinquished.

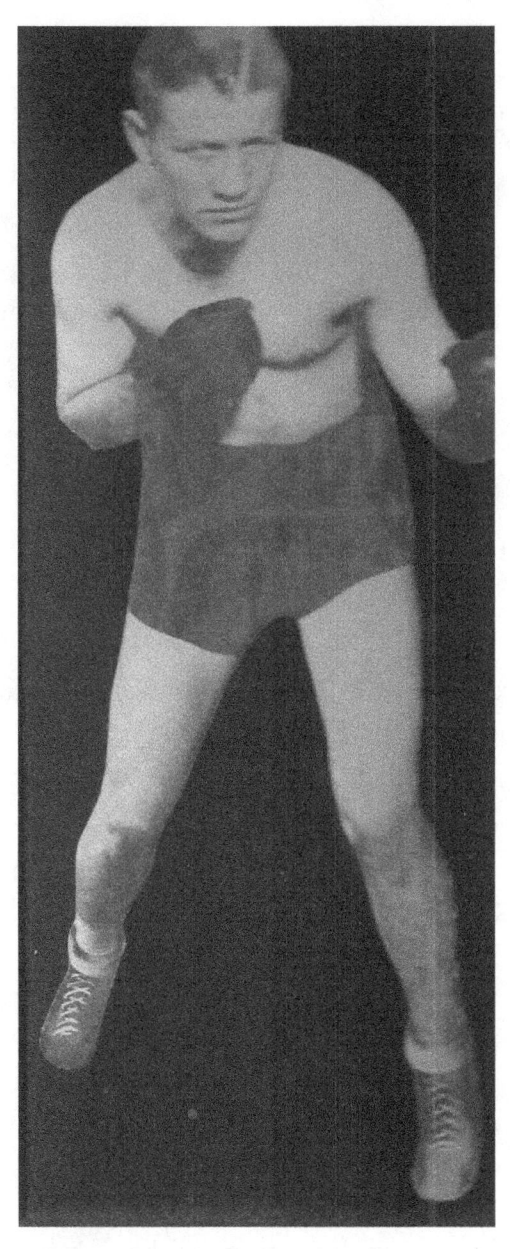

> A financial statement, as nearly as one could gather up from the odds and ends of the talk around the room before the fight was called off would read something like this:
> Deposited to Waxman's account $23,000
> In Donald's account, but attached 13,000
> Check in Waxman's possession 11,000
> Taken in at the gate, cash and checks 25,000
>
> Total in sight, exclusive of money spent $72,000

56& 57 (Ace Hudkins' Scrapbook Clipping)
Finances of the fight.

City Prosecutor, Dr. E. J. Lickley wanted to focus on 3 questions for the commission:

1. Did the Commission have any knowledge of the fact that Waxman had a secret contract with Promoter Dick Donald calling for a $60,000.00 guarantee to be paid in advance?
2. Did the Commission have knowledge that any part of this advance guarantee had been paid to Waxman prior to the evening of the fight? And if so, what did they have to say about it in the face of their own law that no money is to be paid in advance?
3. Why did the Commission, which was present on the evening of the fight and aware of the fact that no fight was going to

take place, not order at once the refund of money to the $2.20 seat purchasers, who were given no stubs to show for the money paid?

58 Coast rocks with fight scandal, a riot of angry fans, and Joe Dundee and promoter Dick Donald were placed under arrest. (Ace Hudkins' Scrapbook Clipping)

59 Ace Hudkins, present and prepared to fight Dundee. Corsica Daily Sun (Corsica, Texas) Thursday November 10, 1927 (International Newsreel, Ace Hudkins' Scrapbook Clipping)

Even Edgar Rice Burroughs, author of the Tarzan books, commented on the event in a letter to his dear friend Herbert T. Weston:

Reseda, Calif. November 10, 1927…We also attended the classical Dundee-Ace Hudkins fiasco last week. You have probably read something of it in the papers.

If all the lousy crooks who make an easy living off the fighters and wrestlers could be eliminated, I think the public might enjoy some pretty good sport, but as it is going now it will not be long before boxing and wrestling will be stopped in California entirely. (Cohen, 2005)

Dundee later claimed that he had not been paid what he was owed, and that was why he did not show. After questioning, Dundee was allowed by Lickley to return east. When attempts were made to re-schedule a fight for April of 1928, Art requested a late May date at the earliest as Ace's hands needed healing after repeated injuries during matches, but it was not to be. Instead, Ace decided to focus on gaining weight in order to box middleweight Mickey Walker.

Dick Donald: Victim or Co-Conspirator?

Donald repeatedly claimed that his enemies were out to get him, which was what led to the problems at the Dundee/Hudkins fight. According to an article by Norman Hartford, there were some interesting factors at play at any rate.

1. Marco Hellmen, L.A. Financier, offered a certified check for $20,000.00 to save the show, which Waxman refused.
2. The State Athletic Commission offered to make up the deficiency—again, Waxman refused.
3. Dick Donald was relieved of duty at Wrigley Field, and there was talk of Jack Doyle taking over. If Donald had asked Field owner William Wrigley Jr for the funds, he surely would have acquiesced, leaving Waxman with no excuse to run out.

Los Angeles Referee Nov. 1927:

"Why the training Ace? Dundee and Waxman have hopped to Baltimore and are indefinitely suspended in California. Whom do you think you're going to fight?"

"Humph. Gotta keep in shape. Goin' to New York in three weeks, me and my three brothers."

"Going to fight Dundee, Ace?"

"Uh-huh if I can get him inside the ropes."

"Do you mean, Ace, you're going to run Dundee ragged, chase him all over the country, until he agrees to fight you…with the championship at stake?"

"You got me pegged right. That's what me and my brothers are gonna do. Gotta keep in shape. I trained six weeks to meet Joe Dundee and then they give me the bird. I didn't even get training expenses. But my time's coming."

The Hudkins had spent a lot of money preparing for the Dundee bout. They trained at Baker's Ranch, and paid sparring partners $15 a day.

To compare, Jack Dempsey spent $1000 a week at Soper's Ranch prepping for Jack Sharkey.

The Hudkins spent $5000 at Baker's.

Immediately following the fiasco, there were talks of Dundee and Hudkins fighting in Tijuana in connection with a racetrack there. The Hudkins had known connections at Caliente racetrack.

60 Clippings from the Olympic Program. (Ace Hudkins' Scrapbook)

HE HAS RUINED the hopes of more championship contenders than any boxer in history.

HE HAD 149 professional fights and does not know what defeat means.

61 Ace Hudkins' Scrapbook Clipping from The Olympic Program.

"What Clyde And Art Hudkins Say"

"The Cat was in the ring and ready to fight. Dundee wasn't and the main reason was because Dundee and Waxman were scared stiff. They knew that Ace would take him like Grant took Richmond if he crawled in that ring last Thursday night at Wrigley Field."

Those are the words of Clyde and Art Hudkins, brothers of Ace.

They continued: "At four o'clock in the afternoon, Waxman came and told us that his fighter had eaten dinner and did not care to go on. He neglected to say anything to us about money matters. If he had, we would have supplied the money ourselves. We would have paid the deficiency just to have gotten the title."

The Hudkins boys believe that they are rightfully entitled to training expenses. They laid out much money for a training camp and for expenses at Baker's Ranch and naturally want it back out of the amount now being held up from the gate sale."

Los Angeles Referee, Nov. 1927 (Hudkins Scrapbook Clipping)

Clyde Hudkins

Clyde Says:

"It's going to be Christmas dinner back in old Nebraska for the Hudkins boys, then a trip to New York City with the big idea of forcing Joe Dundee to fight Ace for the championship. We first will stop in Detroit to tackle some worthy fighter perhaps Jack Zivic. Dundee now is under suspension in California and New York. So is Max Waxman, his manager, all because of the Los Angeles 'walkout' that lost Ace his chance at the crown. Dundee is not worth a dime to anyone until he fights the Wildcat and we intend to stay with him until he does."

Art Hudkins

Art Says:

"I can't say so much because I'm his brother. But I think he is the greatest fighter produced since Benny Leonard.

We figure Ace is a bigger card in New York than Dundee. And we are going to hold out for our guarantee. Of course, we want the title and know Ace will take it away from the Baltimore Italian if given his chance. But we are not going to lose money chasing Waxman and Dundee around when we can draw packed houses anywhere in the country meeting other men."

Courage

Fight to win your heart's great craving

Dare to make your dreams come true

For the world applauds achievement

You can make it come to you!

Work and win- and your endeavors

With success will all be crowned

It's the failure who stops fighting

For the victor can't be downed.

<small>Unknown author of poem found in Ace Hudkins' scrapbook</small>

Extra! Extra!

Ace in Trouble.

Ace, at one time, was suspended in multiple states. He could not fight in Kansas, as their commission had accused him and Clyde of collusion to fix a fight. California found no basis for the complaint and found the accusation came from a disgruntled person on the Nebraska commission. They claimed that Clyde arranged for Ace to fight a former sparring partner in order to have an unfair advantage.

He was reinstated in December of 1927.

Extra! Extra!

Friends of The Wildcat

Ace had many friends and acquaintances. Some were in the boxing world, and some were from the world of entertainment. Among his friends were Jim Corbett, Paul Jones, Dick Spencer, Leo Fonarow, Theodore Kosloff, Harold Matthews, Harry Levine, Jack Dempsey, Helen Tamaris, and Tom Kennedy.

Jim Corbett

62 Jim Corbett and Paul Jones (Author's collection)

"Gentleman" Jim Corbett was also known as the "Father of Modern Boxing." In 1892, he knocked out the great John L. Sullivan and became World Heavyweight Champion. He was the first world heavyweight champion, under the Queensbury rules, when he defeated John L. Sullivan in 1892. In 1942, Warner Bros. produced, and Raoul Walsh directed, a movie of Corbett's life titled "*Gentleman Jim*," starring Errol Flynn, and Ward Bond. Ace worked, uncredited, as an advisor on the film.

Paul Jones

63 Paul Jones (Author's Collection)

Paul Jones was an innovative wrestler and promoter in Atlanta, Georgia. He formed Georgia Championship Wrestling in 1944, under the name of ABC Booking, holding its matches at Atlanta's Municipal Auditorium. "Gorgeous" George Wagner was among those who wrestled at the Auditorium.

64 Back reads: Ace and his pal out to the ranch where we were. [Probably Paul Jones] (Author's collection)

65 Ace in training. (Author's collection)

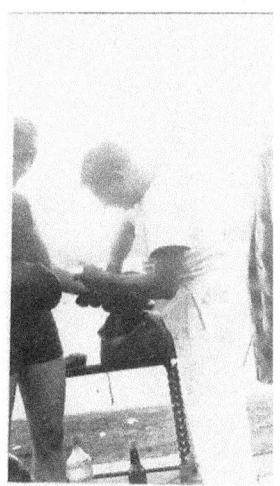

66 Ace training. (Author's collection)

67 Dick Spencer & Paul Jones. (Author's Collection)

Leo Fonarow

68 Leo Fonarow wishes Ace luck against Sammy Baker. (Ace Hudkins' Scrapbook Clipping)

Leo Fonarow, local sportsman, is shown wishing Ace Hudkins good luck a few hours before Ace was due to climb through the ropes with Sammy Baker at Wrigley Field.

Fonarow is a great friend of the "Wildcat." The local sportsman who is proprietor of the Victor Clothing Company, is also chairman of the athletic committee of the Concordia A.C. (Athletic Club), which opens its big gymnasium on August 11. (Ace Hudkins' Scrapbook Clipping)

The Victor Clothing Company dressed Mickey Rooney, Elizabeth Taylor, and Carmen Miranda and the basement, known as the Rainbow Room, was rented out for Hollywood parties. The building later became known for its famous murals.

Theodore Kosloff

69 Ace showing Theodore Kosloff some boxing moves.
USC Digital Library

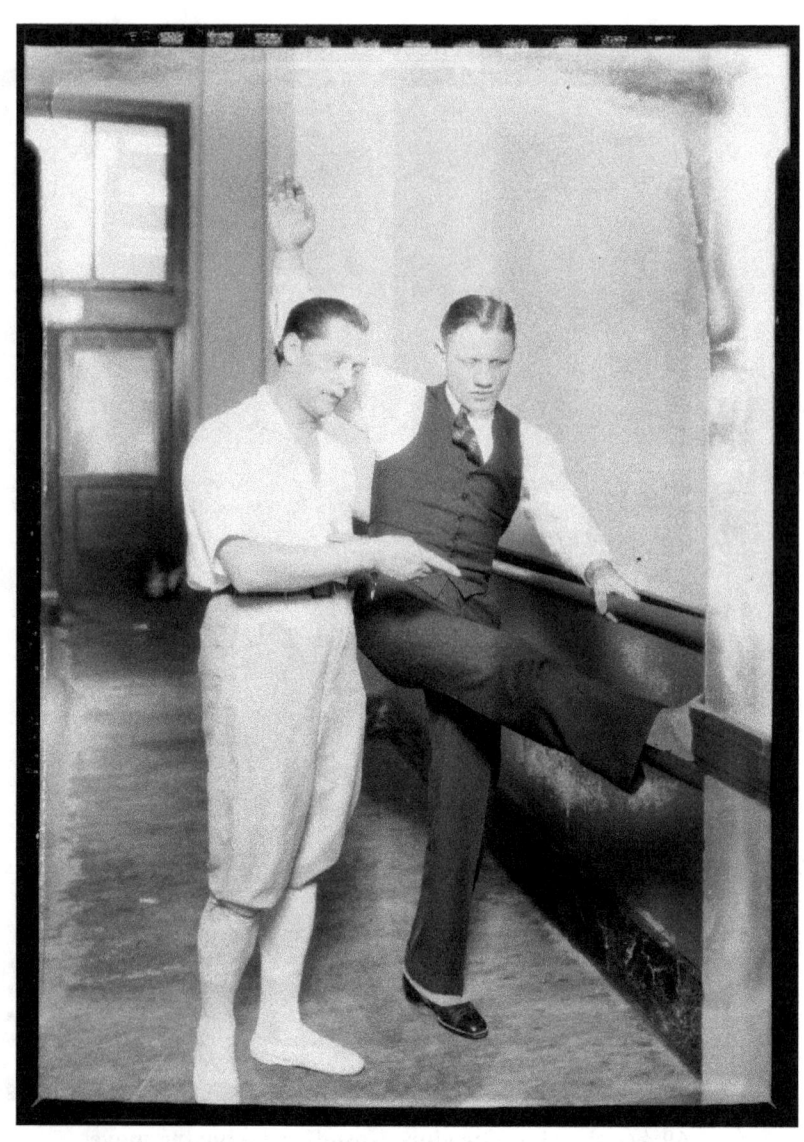

70 Kosloff showing Ace some ballet positions. USC Digital Library

> *Ace Hudkins, known to boxing fans as the "Nebraska Wildcat," decided the other day that a ballet master would be able to help him develop his leg muscles so that he could show faster footwork in the ring. The two pictures... show a couple of incidents as "Ace," who has been signed for a big bout with Lou Tendler at the Olympic, traded instructions with Theodore Kosloff, ballet master. At the left Kosloff is telling the boxer that he should point his toe before he goes any further in his ballet training. At the right Hudkins is showing Kosloff the way a boxer squares off in a ring.*

(Ace Hudkins' scrapbook clipping)

Theodore Kosloff, seen with Ace in the previous photographs, was a well-known choreographer as well as an actor who appeared in such films as Cecil B. DeMille's *The King of Kings* (1927), and *Stage Door* (1934), alongside Katherine Hepburn.

Harold Matthews and Harry Levine

71 Signed: Sincerely, Harold Mathews and Harry Levine

Harold Matthews lived in and fought many rounds in Lincoln, Nebraska from 1928-1935. It is possible that he went into managing and or training Harry Levine when he retired from the ring.

Jack Dempsey

72 Clippng of the great Jack Dempsey! (Ace Hudkins' Scrapbook Clipping)

In January of 1932, it was suggested that Ace Hudkins might meet Jack Dempsey in the ring. Jack Dempsey had this response, *"I'd just as soon meet Hudkins as Dynamite (Jackson). Beside, Ace is sure to draw better. I know Hudkins isn't any knockover but I don't want setups. I want the best fighters in the country."*

Jack Dempsey is known as one of the greatest fighters ever. One of his nicknames was "The Manassa Mauler." He was responsible for the first million-dollar gate.

<u>Dempsey and Ace Help Flood Victims</u>

73 Ace boxing to help flood victims. (Ace Hudkins' Scrapbook Clipping)

March 22, 1928

Jack Dempsey and Ace Hudkins appeared as referees in a charity match for the benefit of those who suffered in a Santa Clara river valley flood.

Helen Tamaris 1905-1966

74 Ace teaching Tamaris some fighting poses for her interpretive dance, "Prize Fight Studies." 1928 International Newsreel photo. (Ace Hudkins' Scrapbook Clipping)

Helen Tamaris, seen with Ace helping her with some boxing stances, was far ahead of her time and explore social issues through the medium of dance – this was considered somewhat risqué in this era. One of the dances she choreographed was of a group of eight Negro Spirituals in a bid to fight against prejudice and discrimination. The dance was entitled *How Long, Brethren?* (1937) and was performed for the Federal Dance project of the WPA. (The Work Progress Administration, was initiated during the Great Depression to put people back to work building roads, etc., and employed artists, dancers, musicians, and writers, etc., to create and promote the Arts.) She also choreographed *Annie Get Your Gun* for Broadway in 1946.

She became the director and was the principal choreographer for the Federal Theater Project under the WPA from 1937-1939.

Jack Sharkey 1902- 1994

75 Ace with Jack Sharkey, joking for the camera.

Tessa/Herald- Examiner Collection//Los Angeles Public Library

Jack Sharkey served in the Navy, and he took his professional name from his two favorite boxers, Jack Dempsey and Tom Sharkey. He fought Joe Louis and Jack Dempsey among many other heavyweights.

Tom Kennedy 1885-1965

Tom Kennedy boxed from 1911-1914 but segued his way into movies in 1915. He was known for playing big, tough, guys. Early in his career, he worked with:

Stan Laurel (*The Egg*, 1922)

Laurel & Hardy (*Liberty*, 1929) (*Pack Up Your Troubles*, 1932) and (*Hollywood Party*, 1934)

The Marx Brothers (*Monkey Business*, 1931)

Later he appeared with:

Bob Hope (*The Princess and the Pirate* 1944)

Maureen O' Hara and Paul Henreid (*The Spanish Main* 1945)

Bob Hope (*The Paleface* 1948)

Tony Curtis, Jack Lemmon and Marilyn Monroe (*Some Like it Hot* 1959)

Spencer Tracy, and a cast of thousands (*It's A Mad, Mad, Mad, Mad World* 1963)

Alongside this, he starred in many tv shows, such as:

The Texan (1959)

Wanted: Dead or Alive (1959)

Bronco (1959)

Sugarfoot (1959-60)

Maverick (1959-61)

Have Gun-Will Travel (1961)

Cheyenne (1959-61)

Bonanza (1961-63)

The Rifleman (1961-63)

Rawhide (1963-64)

Death Valley Days (1964)

Gunsmoke (1964-65)

As you can see, he had a long and distinguished career on film. Many of these programs used horses, wranglers and wagons from the Ranch that the Hudkins ran after Ace's boxing career.

Tom Kennedy was on the scene when Ace signed his second contract to fight Walker and shortly after the fight, on November 13, 1929, the former boxer and screen tough guy purchased Ace's contracts and took over management of his career. It is unclear why the Hudkins brothers decided on this, but it may be because Clyde had previously been against Ace getting involved in the entertainment business. As a former boxer, and current actor, Mr. Kennedy could guide Ace's career in different directions that Clyde may not have been ready to yet approve. Art was Ace's manager at the time of Kennedy's purchase and Ace, Kennedy and the brothers immediately left for Hot Springs, Arkansas.

On June 10, 1930, about seven months after Kennedy took the reins, the brothers bought back Ace's contracts. He had lost three out of four fights by decision since Kennedy taking over, although it is difficult to determine where blame for these losses should be placed. Kennedy had purchased Ace's contracts for $40,000.00, and it was not revealed what agreement had been reached to transfer ownership back to the Hudkins brothers. It is possible, due to the relatively quick turnaround, that the original purchase was more like a loan that was given with the understanding that the brothers would eventually want to buy the contracts back. However, this is conjecture.

Art and Clyde announced that they wanted Ace to pursue Walker's title again.

Extra! Extra!

Hot Springs, Arkansas

In the 1920's, Hot Springs operated as an open town and allowed gambling. It was known for rampant voter fraud and for being a respite for Lucky Luciano and Al Capone.

It was also known as a spa city, and Babe Ruth visited regularly.

76 Souvenir postcard of The "Hudkins Gang" in 1920's Hot Springs, Arkansas. Tom Kennedy, Alphonse? Ace, unknown others, Art and Clyde? (Author's collection)

**77 Souvenir photo of Art and Guests in "Arkansaw"
(Author's collection)**

Wheeler Springs and Soper's Training Camps

78 Clyde and Ace at Wheeler Springs, CA. Jack Dempsey also stayed there while training at Pop Soper's Training Camp, which was close by. (Author's collection)

Clyde and Art as Brothers and Managers

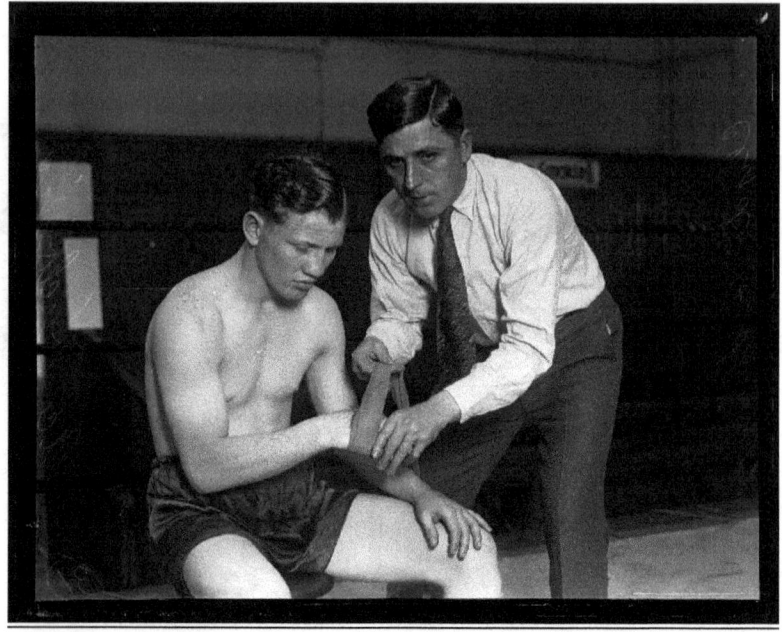

79 Clyde wrapping Ace's hands. Reproduced from the original held by the Department of Special Collections of the Hesburgh Libraries of Notre Dame.

After guiding Ace to the top of the fight game, both Clyde and Art saw an opportunity to manage other young boxers. The author can imagine the line of willing young boxers that stood in a line running out the door of the gym!

CLYDE HUDKINS
Manager of

	Pounds
Ace Hudkins	147
Eddie Mahoney	140
Fred Cullen	160
Tiger Jack Burns	118
Red Humphreys	118
Alphonzo Gonzales	135
Jack Roper	195

Phone OLympic 5152
2302 Observatory Ave.

80 At one time Clyde was managing six fighters in addition to Ace. (Ace Hudkins' Scrapbook Clipping)

81 Paul DeHate joined the Hudkins Stable, under Clyde's management. (Ace Hudkins' Scrapbook Clipping)

82 Holiday greeting, possibly from an Olympic Auditorium program. Also included on the bottom of the greeting, are Charley Long, Tiger Jack Burns and Bobby Fernandez, as part of the Hudkins Stable of boxers. (Ace Hudkins' Scrapbook Clipping)

Alongside Charley Long from Omaha, Nebraska, in 1928 Clyde also managed Jack Thompson and Young Harry Wills. Charley Long boxed the same Sammy Baker in 1928 that Ace had fought in 1927, and knocked out Bert Colima in 1927. Clyde started buying up contracts to the point that some felt he had an unfair monopoly.

"Clyde Hudkins- One of the greatest managers in the game today. "The Wildcat" is a great fighter-but don't forget that this pleasant, smiling and obliging manager had words to do with the Wildcat getting where he is today. Clyde Hudkins is a modest chap- he claims nothing, but Ace Hudkins is a lucky bird in having a brother like Clyde to handle his affairs. I could write columns about why he is a great manager- I could quote what Matchmakers and Promoters have said about him that will bear me out in my contention that he is even a greater manager than Jack Kearns. Ace is a fighter - but without Clyde- he would be like a ship without a rudder. The Hudkins boys are all pals- they stick together like glue, but you'll have to hand it to "Dapper Clyde." He's a great manager and even a bigger and a better asset than the Hudkins boy realizes and which time will only bear me out in my contentions. Clyde Hudkins has the ability, the nature, the manner, the style and everything that goes to make a great manager. He is a great mixer. I'll place him at the very top of all the managers in all the world when it comes to being a good mixer and a popular fellow and I look for Clyde Hudkins to grab a good boy some of these days and with his ability as a manager to

bring that boy to the very top and take him as far as he took ACE and that is to the TOP." (Ace Hudkins' Scrapbook Clipping)

Clipping about the Hudkins Stable of Boxers:

"Here's the Hudkins stable of scrappers snapped by a World-Herald staff photographer during their day's visit in Omaha last Friday. At the left is Art Hudkins, brother-manager of Ace. The little fellow next to Art is Tony Mandell of Worcester, Mass., who has joined the Hudkins and in who Ace has taken much interest. Little Tony is a bantam and is the next champion in this class if he can get a match with Buddy Taylor, the present title-holder, if one is to take Ace's word for him.

In the center is trainer Lewis. Next gent is the Nebraska Wildcat himself. On the right is Big Tony Argento, also of Worcester, who "belongs" to Art. At least Art claims he is a puncher like Paul Berlenbach and will go to the top of the 175-pound division."

On September 2, 1929, Art announced that he had bought the contracts for Leslie "Wildcat" Carter, "junior lightweight," from William Neal. Carter fought Goldie Hess on September 9, at the Olympic and lost by a TKO.

Art Hudkins

83 Art Hudkins. (Ace Hudkins' Scrapbook Clipping)

Art Hudkins Is Developing Stable of Young Boxers.

"Art Hudkins, youngest member of the Hudkins family, spends lots of time getting Ace into trim for his fights but Art is working secretly on some other boys he is developing.

One of them is Bobby Fernandez, hard-hitting Mexican lightweight who Art says will beat his weight in wildcats in a few months. The Hudkins family bought Fernandez's contract for $1,000 two weeks ago. That's how much they think of the boy.

Another boy in the Hudkins stable is Tiger Jack Burns, a Greek who lives in Wilmington. Burns has met and beaten some of the best of them, including Eddie Shea and Midget Mike O'Dowd.

Ancil Hoffman, promoter at San Francisco, is anxious to sign Ace for a bout with Gilbert Attell there this month. It will be an open air show. Fernandez and Burns will fight on this card if financial arrangements are made with Hoffman, according to Art."

(Ace Hudkins' Scrapbook Clipping)

84 Art, Mary and Ace. (Ace Hudkins' Scrapbook Clipping)

> *"Ace Hudkins may be a "Wildcat" in the ring but there is one person who this 22 - year old fighter always remembers, and that's his mother.*
>
> *Ace, accompanied by his brother Art, visited their mother in Lincoln Sunday and expect to visit her again next month when they stop off here enroute to California.*

> *Mrs. Hudkins now lives in a fine bungalow in Lincoln. This house was purchased with the first $7000 Ace earned with his fists while fighting in California.*
>
> *"I have made money with my fists and I may lose all the money I have made, but lose or not, I always have a home I can go to in Lincoln," said Ace."* (Ace Hudkins' Scrapbook Clipping)

Extra! Extra!

The Red Tights

Hudkins has an angle on New York, too.

The big town won't sanction his red plush tights which his mother made for him when he started for California three years ago and said:

"God bless you, Acey. I know I used to have to spank you, but don't let anybody else do it."

She handed Acey a package. It contained a pair of boxing trunks made from her wedding dress.

(Ace Hudkins' Scrapbook Clipping)

January 6, 1928, Ace fought Mike Rozgall in Omaha and won by a TKO. After the fight, he attended a party thrown by the Knights of Columbus. At the party:

"He sang for the crowd and then made the young ladies all anxious to know him more intimately with his grace on the dance floor".

(Ace Hudkins' Scrapbook Clipping)

Extra! Extra!

Ace on Finance and Business

In the early to mid 1920's, Ace started to invest. He began by, buying his mother a house in Nebraska, then he bought a house in Los Angeles, and started various businesses. He bought a cigar store on Seventh street in Los Angeles, and in the 1930's he owned The River Bottom Bar. Together, the brothers bought and owned The New Deal Inn, a diner across from Warner Brothers Studio. In 1949, Ace was also owner of Ace Hudkins Sports Center at 3700 West Olive Avenue in Burbank, CA.

"The Hudkins boys- Ace, Clyde and Art-are now owners of a cigar store on Seventh Street.

They still kid Clyde about smoking White Owls. Down in Nebraska a White Owl is considered a good rope.

Even a tobacco taste changes with prosperity.

They go for the "two-for-a-half" babies now-wholesale and how.

Sure, the Wildcat smokes his "occasional."

Some of the Simon-Pures begin to whisper that Ace isn't taking care of himself when they see him coming down the street smoking a chimney.

Ace has his answer.

"Say, you guys- I ain't no baby in the ring, am I? Some of you fellows baby yourself outside the ring so much you aren't nothin' but babies in the ring. To be tough you gotta be tough, ain't you?"

(Ace Hudkins' Scrapbook Clipping)

...don't think this cat hasn't saved his money. I could quit the ring after Thursday's battle and never worry about where those meals are going to come from. - Ace

"*Ace Hudkins, whose boxing career in the 1920's made him a millionaire, is not one to sneer at the game that made him rich. "I won't knock the sport like a lot of ex-fighters once they've hung up their gloves. It's been good to me," he said.*

A glance at the Hudkins holdings, a North Hollywood motion picture prop rental business, is enough to convince a visitor of his sincerity."

"Fight Game was Good to Ace Hudkins." *The Los Angeles Times,* (Los Angeles, California)

Extra! Extra!

Ace on Funny Business in Chicago

"Too many machine guns there." -Ace

It was well known that the boxing business could be dangerous, not just in the ring but also out of it. Clyde's wife, Katherine, carried a gun to protect Ace's winnings when they travelled, as they often carried the money with them.

Mickey Cohen

It would be a disservice to history, and a disservice to the truth, to say that people such as Mickey Cohen, Sam Giancana and Al Capone had no part in boxing, or entertainment, during the 1920's through the 1940's. Las Vegas itself was built by Bugsy Siegel, who worked for Lucky Luciano and Meyer Lansky. Bugsy was friends with, or seen in the company of, Gary Cooper, Clark Gable, George Raft, Louie B. Mayer and Jack Warner.

The 500 Club in Atlantic City, New Jersey was run by Skinny D'Amato, and such greats as Dean Martin & Jerry Lewis, Frank Sinatra, Jimmy Durante and Nat King Cole all played the club. Martin & Lewis basically owed their careers to their success at the 500 Club.

Owney Madden, known for bootlegging, first hid out, then settled in Hot Springs, Arkansas, in the 30's, becoming a boxing manager and running illegal gambling. George Raft was his driver.

Mickey Cohen worked under Bugsy. He started out as a boxer himself but quickly rose up the ranks as a gangster. When Bugsy Siegel was killed, Cohen took on a much larger role in the L.A. area, running gambling, shake-downs, blackmail, and basically all the rackets. He hired Johnny Stompanato as a bodyguard, who later had an affair with Lana Turner, which resulted in his death. Mickey Cohen ran L.A. There is talk that he ran the movie studio unions and used blackmail to gain cooperation when he wanted it. He was the west coast crime boss after Bugsy died. Ruby Goldstein himself was half owned by bootlegger and gambling kingpin, Waxey Gordon.

Ace On Other Sports

"The Yankees are favored to win the pennant again because they pile in with the old war mace. Ace Hudkins is given a first-class chance to win the welterweight championship against a better boxer because he'll wail away with both gloves, from the first rush to the final episode, win, lose or draw."

- Grantland Rice, comparing what it takes to win, whether it is baseball or boxing.

It is well established that Ace was a winner in the ring. However, he also participated in other athletic activities. During the 1930's he played polo with Darryl F. Zanuck and other Hollywood professionals. There was even a racehorse named after him. So, what did Ace think of other sports?

Golf

Ace headed out on many mornings with friends for a game of golf.

"...what we go out for is the fun of kidding each other. We don't go out to roll up low scores. We can't do it to begin with. But what we don't do is to take the game too seriously. That takes out all the fun-to me at least."

Baseball

Ace spent his afternoons at Wrigley Field in Los Angeles and played three games for the Lincoln Team for the Western league. He organized a team called The Nebraska Wildcats, and they toured in a Cadillac and two Fords, winning 9 out of 12 games. Ace claimed, *"Never had a better time in my life. It was just one long, wild laugh all the way through."*

On June 11, 1928 Ace, Mickey Walker, Jack Kearns and other boxers played on the same baseball team in a game against Chicago sports writers at Mills Stadium. The writers won 17-15.

Extra! Extra!

Lou Tendler

Ace beat Lou Tendler in both 1927 and 1928.

There is a general opinion that The Wildcat took it a little easier on Tendler during the second fight, due to a feeling of sympathy towards him.

1928
The First Walker/Hudkins Fight
What Happened?

"I didn't expect any band. The bands are for the champions. I'll have a band when I leave." -Ace

Walker was met at the station with a band, and Chicago's mayor hosted him while Ace had only a small contingency to meet him.

"I'll knock his block off Morrie. I'll do that for you, kid."

Ace to Morrie Schlaifer, who had lost to Walker previously.

ACE HUDKINS
The Nebraska Wildcat

"I'm going to fight as I have never fought before. I don't want my brothers and sister to see me get trimmed." -Ace

Referring to the 1928 match, Damon Runyan says:

"Ace Hudkins is apt to prove the most difficult opponent Walker has ever faced. (Ace is)...a rip-snorting fighter...his tearing in style is the very thing that may prove his undoing against a superior puncher like Walker. I guarantee that the "Toy Bulldog" will have both hands full all evening."

85 Ace Hudkins and Mickey Walker (AP Photo)

86 The Toy Bulldog verses the Wildcat! (Ace Hudkins' Scrapbook Collection)

"An Eager Champion: Mickey Walker, middleweight champion of the world, and his manager, Jack Kearns, awaiting the bell that will send the champion into battle tonight with Ace Hudkins. both Kearns and Mickey are sure of victory."

Walker said: *"I never make predictions. But I do know I'll be in there fighting as I have never fought before. And there is not going to be a new middleweight champion for the next few months at least."*

"Confident Challenger: Ace Hudkins, challenger, who is certain he will wear the middleweight crown at the close of tonight's fight. Like Walker, Ace is

ready for the gong. If confidence bears any part in the fight the challenger has a big edge."

Ace said: *"It's the greatest chance of my career. I have brought my brothers and sister here and all my friends to see me win this title. I'm not going to disappoint them. I know it will be a great fight. No one ever accused Walker or me of not having fighting hearts. If I answer the bell for the fourth round you can wager the title will change hands."*

87 One is picked to win, the other a wild contender. (Ace Hudkins' Scrapbook Clipping)

"...the past performances and the associations of the boys give assurance that there will be nothing of a refined or uplifting nature to offend the sensibilities of those present when they fight."

Westbrook Pegler-- 1928

Cominsky Park, Home of the Chicago White Sox: June 21, 1928.

 20-30,000 people attended the fight at the ballpark with money coming in at $100,000-$150,000.00. This was a record for audience attendance in the Middleweight Division that would stand for years even though three days of rain and threatening clouds may have kept some away.

 The ring was set up where 2nd base would normally sit -- there was even a band playing jazz tunes for the crowd, and for the 1000 fans from Omaha and Lincoln.

 Hudkins got in close any time he could, which was his favorite way to fight. Walker was bleeding from as soon as the first round and both men had cuts over their eyes by the middle of the fight. Clyde later stated, "Ace hurt his right in the second round and couldn't use it afterwards…Mickey opened up some old cuts over Ace's eyes with back hand flips in the clinches, and we could not stem the flow of gore. Consequently, Ace was blinded."

 A slight sprinkle of rain began to fall in the 7th round, and during the 8th and 9th the rain only increased in intensity, until torrential rains began to fall. During the tenth round, the ring was all but submerged in water and Walker and Hudkins' feet were splashing, as the men tried to get their footing.

Before we move on from what many considered to be the grand moment of Ace's boxing career, the 1928 Walker fight, let's take a moment to look at the lead up to that fight, and the aftermath:

Ace had worked his way up the boxing ladder by defeating Ruby Goldstein, Pat Corbett, Lew Tendler, and Sammy Baker among others. He wanted the title. When he gained weight, he simply moved up in class. The Middleweight title belonged to Mickey Walker, and if that's who Ace needed to beat, that's who he would beat. There were three possible factors that may have influenced the outcome that night: a person named Jack Kearns, a place called Chicago and a force of nature in the form of a torrential downpour of rain.

"There are two ways to beat me and only two. One of them is Jack Kearns. He is 'in' so good in Chicago that we may get a bad decision. Or the other way is for Walker to knock me out one of the first three rounds."

Ace Hudkins- Prior to the 1928 fight.

Jack Kearns

There was one other person that Ace had to beat however, and that was Jack "Doc" Kearns. Kearns was Mickey Walker's manager, and had been Jack Dempsey's manager, until a dispute came between them. One reason for this was that Kearns felt that Tex Rickard stole Dempsey from him. After the dispute, Kearns claimed that Dempsey was still under contract, and that if he fought again, Kearns would be entitled to a percentage. Prior to the 1928 Walker fight, Dempsey commented, "I hope Hudkins knocks out Walker so Kearns will get a second trimming."

It is worth noting that in February of 1927 Kerns was interested in managing Ace. He was in negotiations with Clyde and was willing to go as high as $10,000.00 in 1927, which is equivalent to $139,279.10 today, for Ace's contract. Clyde said that he would take no less than $20,000.00. Could it be that Jack Kearns held a grudge due to letting Ace slip through his fingers?

Did Kearns take revenge by ensuring that the Chicago officials in the 1928 fight would give Walker the decision?

Accusations were made that Kearns had paid off officials in the Walker v Shade bout for the title-- Kearns was well-known to be crafty. One observer went as far as to say, *"Ace should lick Walker, but I doubt if he can lick Kearns."*

There is a story about Mickey Walker facing Paul Swiderski: The 1930 Kentucky Derby was the day after the fight, and they were in Louisville, so attendance was low. Swiderski was clearly winning the bout, with Walker about to be counted out. Kearns would not have his champ beaten by a "lesser" fighter, and, just before certain defeat, Doc

Kearns supposedly had Teddy Hayes, Walker's trainer, ring the bell prematurely, giving Walker time to catch his breath!

Before the 1929 bout Ace accused the shrewd Doc of spreading the rumor that Ace was "on his heels," a jazz-age term that could be taken to mean either about to be beaten, or perhaps down on his luck, financially. In retaliation for the rumor, the Hudkins brothers called the police to a party that Walker attended. It is unknown what the brothers reported, but it is likely, being Prohibition era, that they reported liquor at the party which would have been illegal at the time. Walker said that he had seen Ace around at parties, (or "Whoopee Alley," in Walker's words), so his opinion was, why should someone in a glass house throw stones?

Ace claimed, in an article written by Homer Gruenther after the 1928 fight, that he was afraid that Jack Kearns would beat him (rather than Walker beating him), and insisted that Walker could not beat him 'in one round or forty.' Joe Foley, sports editor of the Chicago Post, openly stated that Ace was robbed, and wondered how much money Kearns had spent and who had received it. Boxing had been given a black eye that night in Chicago, he said, and Kearns had taken care of Walker's title by arranging dishonest outcomes for the previous four years. Foley asked how long the boxing world would stand for a manager manipulating fights like this?

Chicago In The 1920's

Olympic- Grams

By Dean Snyder

Ace Hudkins may not fight Mickey Walker in Chicago.

The Wildcat has made up his mind that when his hand is raised as the new middle weight champion of the world it will be in the country that made his rickety and doorless Ford into a big plush Lincoln.

"What for Chicago!" says the Wildcat. "Too many machine guns there."

Kearns has a similar aversion for New York. It is no longer the Doctor's playground since Tex Rickard chose between him and Dempsey.

(From the Olympic Auditorium Newsletter. Ace Hudkins' Scrapbook Clipping)

"Too many machine guns there." -- Ace

With prohibition in full swing, "businessmen" like Al Capone began to bootleg liquor, provide gambling and prostitution, and protect their territory ruthlessly. The St. Valentine's Day massacre, wherein Capone's competition was gunned down, occurred in Chicago in 1929.

Bullets flying, liquor flowing and jazz playing, it was not a sedate little town in which to hold a small boxing match. Chicago was the Big City, capital B, capital C.

Ace was not in a hurry to fight in Chicago, because he knew that Kearns had connections there. There's no doubt he would much rather have fought in New York where he had been so successful against Ruby Goldstein, and Sammy Baker; or perhaps, Los Angeles, his current home turf. But Chicago it was to be, and the big question was: Did Kearns hold undue influence over the officials there?

Headlines like *"CLYDE VERY SORRY DIDN'T BUY BOSSES",* and *"Bitterly Laments Failure to 'Peddle Ice'"* screamed from Homer Gruenther's sports column in a special dispatch to *The World-Herald*. To be fair, at this time Gruenther was a newspaperman from Platte County, Nebraska and as enthralled with Ace as most Nebraskans were. He later became a special assistant to Presidents Eisenhower, Kennedy, and Johnson.

Gruenther went on to say that, on the day after the fight, 36 sport writers gathered for lunch to discuss what they had seen. 24 of those present declared that Ace had won the match. Eight of those supporters claimed that even so, it was by a slim margin, and not enough to take the title from Walker. Writers from the *New York Times*, the *New*

York Herald-Tribune, the Sports Editor for the Associated Press, and *The Chicago Journal* (among others) felt that the "Ace" was robbed of his victory, and they had been sitting in a position to know – they were in the first two rows. It is interesting to note, however, that most Chicago writers felt that Ace deserved to lose because of his "fouls and rough tactics."

According to Gruenther, the referee, Eddie Purdy, stated that he gave five of the rounds to Hudkins, three to Walker and three were even. He felt that even if Hudkins did foul, his boxing made up for it-- he should have been declared the winner rather than Walker, who, it was felt, was given the win simply because he was defending a title. The two judges selected for this fight were Eddie Klein, a restauranteur, and Harry Carroll, a salesman. Neither of these men seemed to have much experience in the boxing ring so one might well ask why they were chosen.

Gruenther gives a glimpse as to how tense relations were between the fans and the crews of the two camps. The Nebraskans were staying at the Morrison Hotel. When Kearns, Walker and his trainer, Teddy Hayes, were walking by on the way to Kearns' apartment, four inebriated and angry men from Alliance, Nebraska pulled Kearns aside. Kearns blustered that he did not make the decision so why pick on him when he wasn't even in the ring during the fighting. The men accused him of buying the judges but before things got ugly for Kearns, several policemen and Nebraskan Detective, Joe Potach, intervened and stopped a potentially dangerous situation.

According to Gruenther, Tom Dennison was among the fans at the fight. He was infuriated when he arrived to find his front row seat occupied, and ushers did nothing to rectify the situation, leaving him to sit in the twelfth row behind two big men so that he could not see as well as he might have. He still insisted that Ace had won!

The day after the fight, Gruenther said, Clyde and Art were in promoter Mullen's office, stating that they regretted the fact they had not paid off officials as friends had warned them would be necessary for a "fair deal" in Chicago. Never ones to shy away from a good game, Gruenther says, "They (Clyde and Art) spent plenty learning that they could win no money here shooting craps with Chicago sharks, however."

According to *The Lincoln Star*, June 27, 1928, *"The Hudkins brothers are very suspicious of the morals of Chicago's boxing world—quoting such evidence as the sudden shift of odds after the judges were announced..."*

Before the fight, Jack Dempsey stated that Ace needed to knock Walker out in order to win, or the decision would go to Walker regardless of how the rounds played out.

It was agreed among the brothers, according to Gruenther, that Ace would be willing to fight Walker for nothing, either in California or New York, but never again in Chicago. Ace felt that he had gotten the worst deal of his life.

Rain

88 Hudkins and Walker, splashing water at their feet. (Hudkins' Scrapbook Clipping)

The fight took place at Cominskey Park and open baseball field. Exposed to the elements as the rain began to fall, by the end of the fight the men were literally splashing around, losing their footing.

Baseball games are called due to rain, however the gladiators fought on. Art himself declared, "If it hadn't rained Ace would have knocked Mickey down plenty of times." Art said that Ace was unable to get momentum for the finishing punch due to the inch or more of rain with fell during later rounds. Clyde stated, "The rain washed away our chances." How much of an impact the weather had on the fight may never be known but one can't help but wonder what would have happened had they fought on a dry canvas.

According to Gruenther's article, Joe Foley stated that the rain was the best thing that ever happened as it staved off a true riot by cooling off the angry crowd.

> *"If it hadn't been for the rain I know there would have been a riot, because 90 per cent of the spectators thought Hudkins won. I really think that the rain was the only thing that stopped those blood-hungry fans from committing a bit of personal slaughter themselves."*
>
> -Nebraskan fight observer

According to an article by Howard Wolff, Ace stated, "*Say, I couldn't 'a licked him any worse. I'da knocked him out if it hadn'ta rained,*" with Clyde chiming in, "*Sure. Ace is right. You see*

Walker was tiring but the slippery mat robbed Ace of his balance. He couldn't get the old drive. That's all that saved Walker."

In the interest of fairness it could be questioned whether Ace was actually overconfident in this particular case. In order to look at the big picture, we must consider the fact that he may have underestimated Walker's boxing ability. According to Rich Brehm, Ace's nephew, *"They had to watch him anyway, 'cause he was kind of woman crazy. When he'd be at training he was supposed to be on his good behavior. He'd want to go romancing you know and that wasn't good. When you're training for fighting and all that."* Perhaps Ace paid a bit too much attention to the ladies, when he should have trained harder? Hard to believe, but, we may never know.

It seems that many agreed that Ace should have been awarded a win. Davis J Walsh claimed that Ace carried 7 rounds out of 10.

"The decision stunned the crowd of 25,000 to 30,000 spectators, who greeted the verdict with booes and disorder. Some of the experts at the ringside in their tabulation of rounds credited Walker with winning only two and giving Hudkins the shade in five."

--Charles W. Dunkley

"Walker was too strong for Hudkins, a great welterweight, but not yet a great middleweight."

--Damon Runyon-- agreeing with verdict.

"Obviously, earning a draw and getting it, especially with Sinister Jack Kearns aligned with the enemy forces, is as difficult and vain a task as nominating Norris for Republican presidential candidate. Thursday night proved that."

--Sportswriter Frederick Ware (George Norris was a Republican senator who very often voted with Democrats, and supported President Franklin D. Roosevelt, a Democrat.)

89 The judges say Walker won, the crowd says Ace won. (Ace Hudkins' Scrapbook Clipping)

The Walker/Hudkins Bout of 1928

90 The Wildcat (Ace) and The Bulldog (Walker) (Ace Hudkins Scrapbook Clipping)

91 Cartoon illustrating the unhappy fight fan after the Walker-Hudkins fight. (Ace Hudkins' Scrapbook Clipping)

As this clipping shows, the fans were not happy with the finding in the Walker-Hudkins fight, nor were they happy with the state of boxing in general in Chicago. Something didn't seem quite on the up and up.

92 Keeping The Kitty Away. Did businessman judges make the wrong decision? (Ace Hudkins' Scrapbook Clipping)

As these illustrations show, many fans disagreed with having businessmen as judges, and felt they had made the wrong call.

DECISION BOOED LOUDLY BY FANS; RAIN SOAKS RING

Early Thunder Storm Cuts Down Size of Crowd; Fight Is Slug Fest from Start to Finish.

WALKER RETAINS FIGHT CROWN;

CHARGES OF CROOKED DEALING IN WAKE OF ACE HUDKINS' DEFEAT

93, 94 & 95 Some headlines from the Walker-Hudkins fight. (Ace Hudkins' Scrapbook Clipping)

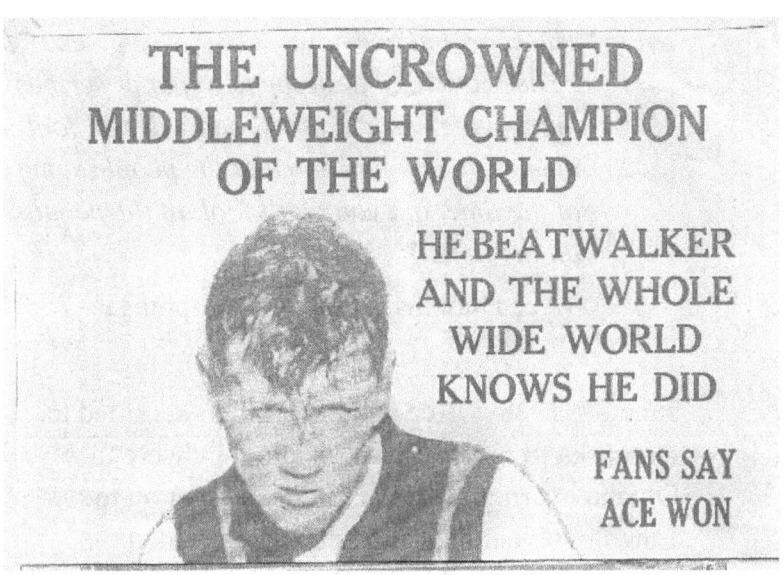

**96 The uncrowned middleweight champion of the world.
(Ace Hudkins' Scrapbook Clipping)**

"Ace Hudkins the Nebraska "Wildcat" who defeated Mickey Walker at Chicago last week. Hudkins took 8 out of the 10 rounds and was given "the works."

Whenever you see ten or fifteen thousand fans say the decision was "rotten", put it down as being just that and nothing else. It makes us laugh to read some of the write-ups by some of the scribes. Can two or three scribes be right when fifteen thousand fans see it otherwise? Can two pair of eyes say it was not right?

The sport public knows "Ace" was given "The Works" and all the newspaper scribes in the wide world cannot, and will not, fool them. You can fool some of the people some of the time, but you can't fool all the people all the time."

(Ace Hudkins' Scrapbook Clipping)

June 27, 1928   Ace and his brothers returned to Nebraska to rest and visit. While they were in Omaha overnight, and before they went on to Lincoln to visit their mother, they attended horseraces at the Ak-Sar-Ben indoor racetrack and were welcomed at the station by a band and several hundred well-wishers.

97 Hudkins boys homeward bound after battle. (Ace Hudkins' Scrapbook Clipping)

> *The House of Hudkins, left to right: Arthur, Albert (Ab), Ace and Clyde.*

> *"One fights; the others boss, but even this combination in which strategy would seem to dominate was unequal to the job of overcoming the deep-laid plans of Mickey Walker and Sinister Jack Kearns in Chicago last Thursday night.*

> *The boys lined up for this picture at the Burlington station this morning, while awaiting a*

train which would take them home to Lincoln and mother. They plan a vacation in Canada and then another fight against Walker – anywhere but Chicago.

The high art of the beautician had rendered Ace's two blue eyes and blow-marked features invisible to the camera's lens. Only two cuts are to be seen, one over each eye." (Ace Scrapbook Clipping)

Upon reaching the Burlington station, Ace was presented with a floral wreath. The Elks band led a parade through town, and a banner, reading, *Welcome home Ace Hudkins, uncrowned champion of the world* flew. Ace finally had the band reception that he was denied in Chicago. Ace said very little about it, but Art declared, *"I'm not mentioning any names but we didn't get an even break on anything from the time we landed in Chicago."*

As Ace rode the parade route, he lifted his cap and waved to his many fans.

Among those present was, warden William Fenton of Nebraska state prison, who had improved conditions at the prison through better food, suits for chapel, a band and a sports team. Also present was, Chief of Detectives (and future Chief of Police) Walter Anderson. He was known as a stickler for department rules, and he modernized the force.

When they reached Mrs. Hudkins' home at 1912 Park Ave., she kissed her boys and shook hands with the many followers who joined them in the parade to her house.

Before entering the house, Ace turned to his followers and said, *"All I have to say, fellows, is that I want to fight Mickey Walker again and I think I can beat him."*

"You've already done it, Ace!" was the reply. There was one more loud cheer from the crowd, and the welcome home was over. Later, a big crowd followed them to the station, complete with bands, trumpets, and cheers!

Meanwhile, back in Chicago, both Kearns and Clyde were suspended, and their Illinois licenses revoked for the infractions of coaching and creating disturbances in their corners. In addition, Kearns was charged with failing to produce Walker at the appropriate time (2 hours before the fight). On Walker's side, Teddy Hayes and Billy Bloxton faced charges, as did Chick Lewis and Sol Gold from the Hudkins' camp.

When the boys returned to California, after a visit in Nebraska, they offered Mickey Walker $75,000.00 and Joe Dundy $50,000.00 to fight in Los Angeles.

Unfortunately, between August 28 and 31, around the time of Ace's 23rd birthday, Ace battled the law instead. He was first caught eluding motorcycle police who caught him doing 60 mph on Pico Blvd., after which he went to San Francisco and on his way home his car scraped a lady's car. Passing motorists stopped him and called for the police. *"Sure, I scraped a fender but it was accidental. These people think I'm drunk,"* said Hudkins. He was taken to a hospital where he participated in a sobriety test-- which he passed, 100%.

Extra! Extra!

Tom Dennison

Tom Dennison was known as "Pickhandle" or "Old Grey Wolf". He ran gambling, prostitution and bootlegging in 1920s Omaha. Having the town in his pocket, he chose who would be elected Mayor, and when his candidate did not win, he incited race riots with false stories in the local paper.

98 Two 'retired' fighters keep on fighting: Tom Dennison and Ace Hudkins. (Ace Hudkins' Scrapbook Clipping)

Ace visiting with Tom Dennison in Nebraska. According to articles of the day, Dennison also visited Ace and stayed with him in California. Claiming not to like to have his photo taken, Dennison said, "*...being that Ace has asked for it, I'm saying yes. Anything that Ace wants that I can give him he can have.*" Ace called Dennison "Uncle Tom" and claimed that after another year of fighting, he was looking to retire.

The Lair of The Wildcat On Observatory

Ace was doing very well financially in the 1920s. So much so, that he was able to buy his mother a house in Nebraska and invest in various businesses. His most prized possession, however, might be the home he provided on 2302 Observatory in the Los Feliz area of Los Angeles. In the 1930 United States Federal Census, Clyde is listed as head of household with his wife Katherine and son Acey, along with Ace, Albert (Ab), and Art, living together under one, well-to-do roof. By the time Acey Hudkins passed away on May 31, 2007, there had been a Hudkins family member living in that house since before 1930.

99 House on Observatory. (Author's Collection)

100 & 101 The Hudkins family home on Observatory, near Los Feliz. (Author's Collection)

102 Ace with Clyde's son, his nephew Acey, born 1927. (Author's Collection, from Ace's Scrapbook)

103 Katherine, Ace, Art and friend after the beach (Author's Collection, from Ace's Scrapbook)

1929

Extra! Extra!

Ace stories:

I Knew You Looked Familiar!

Hudkins was working out in a gymnasium, and brother, Clyde, was deploring the lack of sparring partners. A bystander with a sense of humor, pointed out a husky youth standing in a corner and Clyde rushed over to him.

'I'll give you $11.50 to box a couple of rounds with Ace,' he offered.

'Gosh, thanks, I'd like to,' responded the boy, *'but I can't do it. I'm fighting him in a couple of nights. My name's Belanger.'* Clyde nearly fainted.

Roche, Frank. "Meet the Nebraska Wildcat!" *The Arena* Oct 10, 1929: 35.

The Moral Of The Story Is: Think Before You Answer

Ace was invited to give a radio talk and somebody asked him, *'Is it true that your recent victory over*

Armand Emanuel was one of the easiest fights you ever had?'

Ace considered a moment, and answered, *'Well, I hadn't given it much attention, but now that you mention it, I believe you're right.'* And he went on to explain why he had won ten out of ten rounds against the lawyer-fighter.

"Pa" Emanuel, father and manager of the young light heavy, happened to be listening in on the Hudkins talk, and rushed right up to the broadcasting station. He delivered a great oration, in public, defaming the Hudkins name and abilities, according to bystanders. Hudkins stood just so much, then said:

'Listen, you, if I didn't respect gray hairs I'd punch you right in the snoot.'

Roche, Frank. "Meet the Nebraska Wildcat!" *The Arena* Oct 10, 1929: 35

Between the June 1928 Walker match, and the October 1929 Walker match, Ace had six matches, winning five. Of the five, one stands out in particular: it took place at Dreamland Auditorium in San Francisco on June 28, 1929, and was against Charley Belanger. It seems that the fight was slow. Suspiciously slow. Fight fans hurled their programs into the ring in disapproval. The $20,000.00 purse was held, pending an investigation. If there is one thing we can say about Ace's fighting, as his opponents can attest, he never lays off. If anything, he rushes in and keeps on rushing. In response to allegations that Ace "took it easy," he said:

"You never saw me put up a bad fight, did you? You never saw me stall with anybody did you? I always punch, and punch hard, whenever I have a chance, don't I? This guy hung on and ran. He grabbed my arms and pinned me down. I didn't have a chance to swing a fist. He's a light-heavyweight, and I'm a middle. He hung all his weight on me. I got the decision, I know, but if I ever get another chance at that guy, I'll murder him. I'll hit him so hard he'll be too dizzy to hang on, then I'll knock him out."

"Meet the Nebraska Wildcat!" *The Arena* Oct 10, 1929

The court vindicated Ace and decided that nothing crooked was going on. Now, because of his suspension in New York, and due to California's commission temporarily cancelling his fight with Joe Anderson, Ace needed to be patient.

The Las Vegas Option

104 Ace and Art in Las Vegas, NV. (Film transparency of Ace Hudkins Posing with Men, Las Vegas, 1929, Elton and Madelaine Garret Photo Collection, UNLV University Special Collections &Archives.)

Las Vegas. That name conjures up so many pictures-- lights, showgirls—maybe some think of gangsters. But this was before Las Vegas was *Vegas*. It is hard to believe now, but Vegas was once a desert town, trying to draw tourists. This was before the Flamingo, where Bugsy Siegel ruled through intimidation. This was *way* before the Sands, where The Rat Pack of Frank Sinatra, Dean

Martin and Sammy Davis Jr. ruled through music and laughs.

There was talk about a re-match taking place in Las Vegas on the 4th of July, and plans were put in motion, with Kearns and Tom Kennedy both showing interest. The Hudkins' came to Las Vegas by train in January. Both fighters signed, as of February 1929, but the match never materialized.

LAS VEGAS BACK OF FIGHT PLAN

Town Near Boulder Dam Pulling On Bit For July 4 Bout.

By Victor G. Sidler.

LAS VEGAS, Nev., April 1-(AP)- Visions of future growth with the great Boulder dam in the offing have placed Las Vegas boosters whole-heartedly behind preparations for a proposed championship fight July 4 between Mickey Walker, middleweight king, and Ace Hudkins, "wildcat" challenger from Nebraska.

Blooming almost overnight into flowered prosperity under the prospect of great stores of waters behind a towering buttress across the Colorado river canyon, Las Vegas placed itself behind Tom Kennedy, Los Angeles promoter, who came here with plans for a 20-round titular battle. He has selected the site for a great arena, on the outskirts of Las Vegas, capable of seating 60,000.

Town Near Dam Site.

It is within 28 miles of the shores of the turbulent Colorado, and the Boulder dam site, at Black canyon, upon which the residents of Las Vegas are building hopes of a prosperity that many prospectors failed to unearth in their search for bonanza fields.

Although Las Vegas is situated far from the large metropolitan centers on the coast and the larger cities of the Rocky mountain region, backers of the proposed fight anticipate success in the venture. The title bout would be a re-match the two having met in Chicago last year, at which time Walker won a decision unpopular to many.

Hudkins Pulling Card.

Hudkins always has been a good drawing card [bringing in crowds], *and Kennedy expects fight fans from the Pacific seaboard to help fill his arena.*

Surrounded on all sides by mountainous country that is covered with sage and mesquite, Las Vegas itself is a typical frontier town. Like many of the pioneer communities, it was built up along the railroad, the main street running parallel with the tracks of the transcontinental line. To the city bred person, the country neighboring Las Vegas appears as a desolate waste, with its dusty, gray soil.

The Lincoln Star (Lincoln, Nebraska) Mon, April 1, 1929 Page 12.

105 Ace sparring in Las Vegas with Art in the background. (Film transparency of Ace Hudkins, 1929, Elton and Madelaine Garret Photo Collection, UNLV University Special Collections &Archives.)

106 Ace with Las Vegas Mayor Fred Hesse. Film Transparency of Ace Hudkins, 1929, Elton and Madelaine Garret Photo Collection, UNLV University Special Collections &Archives.

Before it could be scheduled, the National Boxing Association demanded that Walker put up $10,000.00 as a guarantee against forfeit because he had refused to defend his title as often as was required. In other words, if the fight was scheduled, and Walker backed out, he would be required to pay $10,000.00.

There was trouble with the check. It was sent to the Association headquarters in New Jersey rather than to California, where it should have been received.

In the end, Ace fought Anderson in September and waited his turn for Walker.

Extra! Extra!
Las Vegas Mayor J. Fred Hesse
Fred Hesse was Mayor of Las Vegas during Prohibition, however, he was not a big supporter of it. He was once arrested for operating a still.

Extra! Extra!
All about Ace!
"Hudkins has his own car, a house backed up against the Hollywood hills four beautiful dogs-he's very fond of animals-and every convenience that money can buy… Hudkins' career has been meteoric."

Roche, Frank. "Meet the Nebraska Wildcat!" *The Arena* Oct 10, 1929: 14-15

"He gives no quarter and he asks none. He will fight anybody and he is superbly confident that he can beat anybody in the world."

Roche, Frank. "Meet the Nebraska Wildcat!" *The Arena* Oct 10, 1929: 15

Speaking of Sports
By George Kirksey

Mickey Walker, middleweight champion of the world, will enter a ring at Wrigley Field on October 29 to defend his title in a ten-round bout with Ace Hudkins, Nebraska "wildcat," who rules the fistic backyards of Hollywood.

The two slugging battlers will face each other in an atmosphere charged with intense rivalry as the result of one of the most bitter pre-fight barrages ever heard in Southern California.

The "Wildcat" started it as the fighters posed for talking movie cameramen during the ceremony at which signatures were exchanged.

Hudkins made the customary bally-hoo to the effect that the assembled multitude was listening to the next middleweight champion of the world and wound up with an apparently innocent remark.

"I hope," said the Ace with a broad grin, "that Walker will be in condition for this fight. At any rate, he had better be."

Walker, awaiting his turn at the "mike," appeared in favor of starting the battle at once, but cooler heads ruled, and the champion made his little talk.

"The last thing Hudkins has to worry about is my condition," Mickey declared. "However, he'd better be able to take care of himself."

This pleasant exchange, it was apparent, centered about the fact that Walker, on a recent nocturnal trip through the movie center, celebrated with such vigor that he and four companions were finally arrested for fighting in the apartment of a young film actress.

…"I'll admit I play once in a while after a tough fight," Walker declared. "But don't think I'm not ready when I enter a ring. I may have made some poor fights but never because I was out of condition."

Walker also declared that as far as Hudkins is concerned, the "wildcat" lives in a glass house.

"Hudkins is no angel," the champion averred. "He's got the luck, however. He goes on a party and nothing happens while I land in a police station my first night out in Hollywood."

…Walker and Hudkins met a year or so ago in Chicago and the champion too the decision in a heavy rainstorm. Each fighter claims the rain acted against him.

Since the Chicago meeting, Hudkins has changed his style to some extent. He hits harder than previously and uses a little judgement in his rushing tactics.

Mickey, however, claims Hudkins still comes in "wide open" and predicts this habit will result in Ace taking the count.

"Hudkins may have knocked out Joe Anderson by rushing him in their recent fight," Walker said, "but if he comes at me like he did Anderson the fight won't last long."

The Times (Munster, Indiana) 22 Oct. 1929, Tues, Main Edition, page 20

1929

Mickey Walker Versus Ace Hudkins: The "Black Tuesday" Re-match!

October 29, 1929

Wrigley Field, Los Angeles, California

After their last match in 1928, which ended in a split decision, Ace might have asked himself: "What comes next?" The answer was a re-match-- Ace wanted the title. What better way to assure his place in boxing history, than to fight the best? He had fought Walker, the "Toy Bulldog," in June of 1928, and now it was almost a year and a half later.

The fight was set for October 29, 1929. He had fought the greats: Lew Tendler, Sammy Baker, Al Mello, Pat Corbett, Ruby Goldstein, and Mushy Callahan, to name but a few. He had never been knocked out. He *should* have been known as the best of the best, but there was a cloud hanging over his career: that match in 1928 against Walker, which resulted in a split decision.

Ace summed it up best this way in a San Bernardino County Sun interview:

... he [Ace] felt that the coming battle was the big spot in his career in that he had missed three chances to be a champion. 'Sammy Mandel stayed out of my alley when I was a

lightweight....Joe Dundee never showed up when I was at Wrigley Field two years ago to fight him for the welterweight title, and I think I beat Walker in Chicago'

Both sides started the 1920's version of trash-talking as they prepared for the fight. Hudkins said, *"I expect Walker to make it tough for me the first three rounds. After that I'll annihilate him- maybe I'll score a technical knockout by eight rounds. I'm in the best shape of my life and if I lose there will be no alibis."* Walker came back with, *"Anybody who faces Hudkins is in there with a rough fighter. I've trained twenty-five days for this fight and if I never win another fight in my life I want to take this cocky Wildcat. I don't like to predict a knockout, but this fight may be over inside six rounds."*

Ace's mother, Mary, was there, all the way from Lincoln, Nebraska, as were his brothers Clyde, Ab and Art. The brothers had asked for, and obtained permission to be in their brother's corner. Mary would stay at the house on Observatory and listen to the fight on the radio.

What she heard was the last thing that she wanted to hear. Ace charged in gamely round after round, but each time the "Toy Bulldog" beat him back. Ace became increasingly fatigued-looking, while Mickey appeared to be in the pink. Ace was awarded only one round.

One thing we must remember when discussing Ace's boxing history is that he was down, but he was never out.

"I admit I am a tough fighter, but I am a fair fighter. I have only lost one fight on a foul, and I think the referee was wrong on that occasion. I have heard that the Walker people claim I am a foul fighter. They know better, but if they say I am rough they are right. What is this fight thing, anyhow, a pink tea party? They say I am too uncouth for New York, but you may have noticed that it is the rough and ready guys who attract the dough to the box office. Walker says I am on my heels. Well, he will be on his back inside of six rounds and that's that."

-- Ace Hudkins,   Oakland Tribune (Oakland, California) Tues., Oct 29, 1929

October 29, 1929

The Market Crashes, and Ace Hudkins and Mickey Walker Fight

On October 29, 1929, America experienced its' biggest financial blow up to that point. It was called "The Great Crash of 1929" and it began on Thursday October 24 and culminated on October 29th, which was thereafter known as "Black Tuesday."

People had been living high during the 1920s, buying up stocks as they became available. But with unemployment rising and production declining, stocks lost their value. As stock prices declined, people began to panic and tried to sell their stock in the hope of salvaging some of their cash. Soon, the market collapsed completely, leaving those who owned stock completely ruined financially. Thousands of millionaires were suddenly penniless.

It was in this atmosphere, on "Black Tuesday" itself, that Ace arrived at Wrigley Field ready to fight in front of a crowd of between 21,370 to 25,000 fans, depending on the account.

Ace arrived at 8:30 and was not pleased when Walker showed up at 9:30 causing the fight to start fifteen minutes late. This may have been strategy on Walker's part as who could forget what happened with Joe Dundee? The longer Ace had to wait, the more steam he lost.

Jack Kearns, Teddy Hayes and Johnny Forbes were in Walker's corner, while Clyde, Art, Chick Lewis, and Joey Greenberg were in the Wildcat's corner. Lieut. Jack Kennedy was the referee. From the start, Walker focused on body blows, tagging Ace as he rushed towards him, content to let Ace come to him. In the fourth round, Walker cut Ace's left eye. In the seventh and eighth rounds, Mickey was tiring, and Ace was slashing, saying "I got him, Jack!" At one point, Art and

Clyde urged Ace to try body blows on Walker, which worked in his favor and resulted in the only round he won. Except for that seventh round, it was a decisive victory for Walker and he was awarded six rounds, three rounds were found even, and one round was awarded to Ace. As Ace shook Walker's hand, the Wildcat, covered with blood, approached the microphone and said, "I'm glad that's over."

It was as if Ace was thinking that he had worked hard, earning his way fight after fight, only to reach the top and have his chance but failing to walk away with the big title. Would he be able to reach those heights again? Would it be worth it? The blood sweat and tears to make it to the very top were a high price to pay.

On the other hand, how many have attained those heights? Many would have, and did, quit long before they had a chance to realize their dream, whether it be boxing or the top of any profession. Since he had been a child, Ace knew nothing other than hard work. Did he get tired? You bet. Did he get injured? Yes. Did it stop him? Never. Hours, days and years of training brought him to this moment, and he had gone the distance.

If there is anything to be learned from Ace's career, we must remember this: he was never knocked out. He stood up after each punch. Not many people, fighters or not, can say that they got back up after each setback and kept going.

The Day After

The Oakland Tribune said:

All Hudkins has left is heart and he has plenty of that. No gamer fighter ever stepped into anybody's ring. From gong to gong he rushed madly in and always into an inferno of right and left smashes to the head and body. When the going was toughest the Wildcat fought his hardest. There was no method to his campaign. He simply plowed in and was met with cruel punishment by a fighter whose battle had been carefully planned by the most astute of all fight managers, Jack Kearns. Wed., Oct 30, 1929 Page 17.

The Los Angeles Times said:

Nobody but Hudkins, with the heart of a lion, would have survived Walker's punishing blows and retained his feet, but upright he stayed, and each time came back with rallies of his own.

"Come on and fight, come on," was his snarl as, badly hurt, he surged forward with lowered head and invited the champion to slug it out with him.

Wed., Oct. 30, 1929 Page 1

Ace was true to his word, and he offered no alibis after the points said that he had lost. There was no "poor me," attitude; that was not Ace's style. Besides, it had been a great ride, and Ace was still 24 years old. What now? The roller-coaster, just like the ones on Coney Island, had just begun! The adventure would continue…

107 The brothers Hudkins (Author's Collection)

First Steps After The Walker Fight

108 Art, Ace, Morrie Cohan, Fon and Clyde (Ace Hudkins' Scrapbook Collection)

Ace Hudkins (left) and Morrie Cohan, Pasadena boxing promoter. Cohan is giving a big show to raise funds for a dinner for the newsboys. Hudkins plans to return from the east in time to offer his services in an effort to help the show. (Scrapbook clipping)

Morrie and Ace- are above in Morrie Cohan's new Pasadena arena, which is packing in crowds of fight fans every week. Morrie, on the right, had Ace Hudkins as a guest when he gave a benefit show Thanksgiving Day.

Morrie has more millionaires in his Pasadena audience than any arena in the world except Madison Square Garden. He lines up slam-bang fights and a boy must be a crowd pleaser to show at Pasadena. In the above picture, notice how the "Wildcat" is dressed- spats and everything. (Scrapbook clipping *)*

Morrie Cohan was a promoter who often presented charity events. In addition to the above event for injured boxers, Cohen put on an annual Christmas benefit providing Christmas dinners for all the newsboys in Pasadena, CA.

Ace fought an exhibition to benefit the newsies in December of 1929. It was the first time he had stepped into the ring since the Mickey Walker fight.

Morrie Cohan later entered the movies, performing from 1931 – 1939, playing referees, and chauffeurs in movies such as: *I'm No Angel*, with Mae West and Cary Grant, *Belle of The Nineties*, with Mae West, *The Milky Way* with Harold Lloyd and *The Crowd Roars* with Robert Taylor.

Ace Quotes:

Ace Hudkins says the minute rest between rounds should be canned out of the rules...And that the boys should fight until one of 'em drops.

"Hooks and Slides" *The Daily Tribune* 27 Dec. 1928

The Millionaire and the Peasant

There were other fights, such as with Rene De Vos on December 28, 1928. Ace needed to beat the Belgian De Vos if he wanted a shot at the Middleweight title. Anthony J. Drexel Biddle, Jr., was the millionaire manager of De Vos. Biddle courted Hudkins, but when a fight date was set, suddenly developed a boil on his neck and postponed twice. De Vos being managed by a millionaire, led journalist, Westbrook Pegler, to negatively compare Hudkins to De Vos by saying that Hudkins was "*a peasant who cuts his own hair, eats toast out loud and fans soup with his hat.*"

The crowd at Madison Square Garden held more than 19,000 fans who watched Hudkins defeat De Vos.

However, Biddle held an attitude of "nobles oblige," and held a late supper only hours after the fight. Attending the supper at the Hotel St. Regis were: Ace, Police Commissioner Grover A. Whalen, President of The Madison Square Garden Corp., James Bush, Vice President of M.S.G.C., Colonel John Hammond, and Anthony Biddle's father Major Anthony J. Drexel Biddle Sr., as well as hundreds more. Ace and Rene sat at the same table, and amicably chatted, and Biddle Jr. agreed with the outcome of the fight.

Extra! Extra!

109 Illustrating that Ace had to get through DeVos to get to the title bout. (Ace Hudkins' Scrapbook Clipping)

Here's Mr. Ace Hudkins, who, so Westbrook Pegler says, is decidedly a "peasant who cuts his own hair, eats toast out loud and fans soup with his hat."

Mr. Hudkins, who hails from Lincoln, Neb., demonstrated the reasons why he is called the Nebraska wildcat when he traded punches Friday night with Rene Devos, Belgian middleweight, and came through with enough points to win a decision over the protégé of Anthony J. Drexel Biddle, Jr., New York millionaire sportsman. (Ace Hudkins' Scrapbook Clipping)

110 Ace cavorts in training to go against DeVos. Hurdles two sparring partners, Spike Webb and Bob Bolen. (Ace Hudkins' Scrapbook Clipping)

111 Hudkins, the "peasant" was able to win over a millionaire's protégé!

It seems a peasant was able to win over a millionaire's protégé!

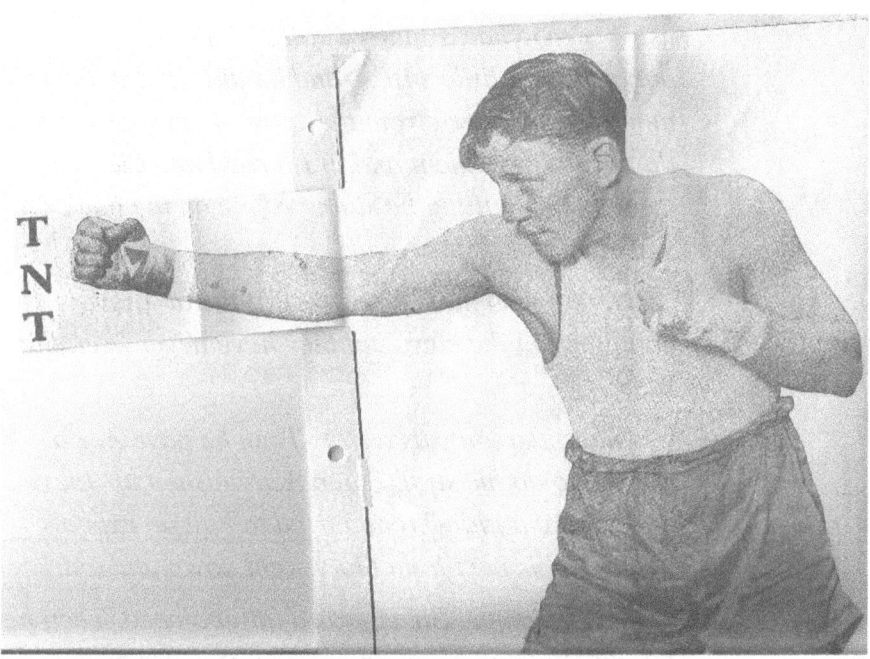

112 "C'mon, let's go to town!" is the Wildcat's battle cry. (Ace Hudkins' Scrapbook Clipping)

Who would blame other fighters for being nervous to step into the ring with The Wildcat?

If Ace doesn't outslug 'em to victory his ripping, tearing methods leave the winner with nothing but aches and pains from which they never recover...

(Joe Benjamin) had toyed with other cyclonic attacks... "I thought I had a sucker, but I drew a cage full of wild animals. He started off shooting for my body and every time he landed I thought he was using a crowbar. Finally I said, 'scatter your punches, you little stiff' – and he did. He hit me almost everywhere from the soles of my shoes to the dandruff department and, if I turned and did something scuttling he slammed me on the back." It was Benjamin's last fight.

Others who have faced the "Wildcat" have continued in the ring- but they have never been the same.

Joe Anderson was a star. Then he gave Ace a chance to do his stuff. When Ace finished up Joe looked like a lad who had tried to halt an express train. In his next fight (Joe) went down and out.

Sergt. Sammy Baker was a lallapalooza. Then he fought Hudkins a few times. He has never been the same slashing, dashing Sammy Baker since then- and he never will be.

Ace pounded Ruby Goldstein off the heights with a few punches at a time when Ruby was new York's most sensational lightweight.

When the first bell rings, the "Nebraska Wildcat" sallies forth with the idea of chasing the other fellow through the ropes, and right out of the arena.

If the fighter decides not to leave the ring that's his bad luck. For Ace, now greatly angered by the refusal to "beat it," proceeds to throw punches from here, there and everywhere, with the prime purpose of having them find lodgement in the other fellow's amidships region.

...whether he hits or misses he keeps on swinging, so much to the everlasting discomfort of the poor lad who thought he was going to fight one man with TWO hands, only to learn that he has drawn a sort of fistic centipede.

Frank G. Menke, Sportswriter for William Randolph Hearst (Ace Hudkins' Scrapbook Clipping)

ACE HUDKINS RUINS ALL THE FIGHTERS

"The Wildcat" has fought in every division up to light-heavy and in each division he has practically ruined a fighter. Hudkins fought as a flyweight in Nebraska- he then jumped to the bantams and when he hit Los Angeles he was a lightweight. I'll let

my good friend Stub Nelson tell you about "THE KITTY." He has followed him pretty close and will give you a big earful of what Ace has accomplished. Stub says:

Nearly every good fighter who has faced the "KITTY" has slowed down afterward.

Ace and the Hudkins troupe rattled into town in an old flivver just as the four-round game was passing out back in 1924.

Before long young Hudkins, waiting 130 pounds, was in action against Dick Hoppe in a four-rounder at the Hollywood American Legion stadium.

That bout -staged by Tom Kennedy - brought eating money and started the "Wildcat" on his winning ways.

Not so long after the 10-round legalized boxing bill went into effect.

One of Hudkins' first opponents was Tommy Carter- in a bout billed for the Pacific Coast lightweight crown. The terrific whirl of the Hudkins attack engulfed Carter. Clever as he was Tommy receipted for a cruel lacing. That was the end of Carter's boxing days. I think you can check me up on that by asking Carter. Tommy, once a fine fighter and now a fine little fellow, is working for the city.

Not so long after came the "natural" with Joe Benjamin out at old Vernon.

Sheikish Joe had long been one of Vernon's standard attractions. He reigned along with Danny Kramer, Young Brown and Bert Colima.

Hudkins gave Benjamin a fearful lacing.

Ever mindful of his looks, Joe hung up the gloves after that one.

THERE WAS SOMETHING IN THE HUDKINS ATTACK THAT KEPT THE MEMORY LINGERING ON.

Hudkins Put Ruby Goldstein on the Skids

Then the New York invasion.

Ruby Goldstein was the toast of the Bronx. A coming champion, his admirers claimed.

Goldstein- a terrific puncher but a cap with a bad chin- knocked the "Cat" down.

That was his mistake. Ace got up- claws extended- and stopped Ruby. Goldstein has done all sorts of queer things since. They have tried to rebuild him- because of his following and popularity- but he doesn't seem to be the same Ruby.

Phil McGraw and Stanislaus Loayzn were also victims of the Hudkins barrage on that trip.

Both of these lightweights were tough- McGraw, the Greek "iron horse," and Loayzn, the Chilean rubber man. But they started downgrade after their evening with the untamed "Kitty."

Sammy Baker isn't the welterweight he once was. His fadeaway is laid to three battles with Ace. He scored in the first bout- but lost the next two. In each bout the boys finished looking like they had used knives.

Now the names of several welters- Jackie Fields, Young Corbett, Young Jack Thompson- all overshadow the army sergeant.

Mushy Callahan felt the "Kitty's" claws. Part of his recent setback must also be charged to Baker.

Al Mello- who knocked out Eddie Roberts in a punch and gave great promise- was practically ruined by the Ace. He never rose to the heights after two battles with the Nebraskan.

Bill Flynn had Billy Atkinson going good out here. They tossed Ace and Atkinson into the Olympic ring. That was Billy's finish in the bog clubs. Ace knocked him back to Kansas.

Billy Ager, the Arizona "iron man" and a chap who fought something like 50 battles in a year, was never down until Ace bounced him off the Olympic floor early in 1927.

While we are about this business- how about Herman Auerbach the Salt Lake kid wasn't a bad looking fighter until he ran afoul of the "Cat." Hudkins put him on a greased toboggan.

Bert Colima has never been the same brilliant performer since he tried to make 150 pounds for Ace at Wrigley Field a year ago last spring.

Colima gamely stood up under a terrific body beating in the last four heats, but those punches still hurt.

<u>They Say Mickey Walker Fears the "Cat"</u>

And don't forget Mickey Walker- the present middleweight titleholder, whom many unprejudiced boxing men say lost to the "Wildcat" in Chicago last June.

The word is out that Jack Kearns has placed such an exorbitant demand for a rematch purse because Mickey fears Ace.

Those prohibitive terms- 100 "grand" and the like- would indicate as much.

"There's one guy the "cat" can knock out," said Brother Clyde last night. "We are going to force that Walker into a fight.".

"Here's another thing to put in your paper. Two weeks after we are through with Anderson we will take Dave Shade. And two weeks after that they can bring on Rene De Vos. We'll fight right through the challengers and then make Walker give us a championship shot or retire from the middleweight ranks."

Clyde went right on to say that Ace is ready for the toughest.

"Ever since Ace fought as a flyweight in Omaha, we have met the best men in every class. That still goes."

By Stub Nelson, Sport Editor, L.A. Record.

Hudkins looks better in the gymnasium now than ever before. He is a great fighter at this weight- you will see a savage and strong fighter when Ace goes to the post against Anderson. It was only a few weeks ago that he "Cat" was weighing 165 pounds- he works when he trains- he looks perfect right now and the only thing I can see that will keep him from stopping Anderson is the fact that he has been idle for a long spell while "Kentucky Joe" has been fighting and is in real fighting form.—Van, Editor

(Ace Hudkins' Scrapbook Clipping)

The Wildcat Has A Rough Spell

Ace continued to fight until 1932, sometimes winning, sometimes losing, but one thing is for certain-- he had quite a ride. Between the Walker Fight in 1929 and his final pro match in 1932 he lost as many as he won. On July 31, 1931, Ace was arrested for drunk driving and crashing into a parked car. On January 11, 1932, Ace was arrested after he fractured a man's skull. It seems Ace's companion, Ellen, had been honking the car horn at two men, and when they objected Ace got out and knocked them both down. Another report of the incident says that Ace and Ellen were standing at an intersection when the men were rude to Ellen. Ace was held for assault with a deadly weapon-- the deadly weapon being his fist. Ace was sued for $50,000.00, but the plaintiff was awarded $1.00. On March 25, 1932, Ace was sued for $100,000.00 for breach of promise by a different woman, and $60,000 for allegedly striking the same lady. On April 1, charges were dismissed.

In 1933, Ace's last professional fight with Wesley Ketchell ended with Ace losing by points, however he was as tough a fighter as ever, because it turned out that he had three cracked ribs! Ace told reporters that it felt like nothing worse than a toothache. On February 19 of 1933, while Ace was staying at The Aloha Rooms Hawaii, and was arrested for possession of okolehao, a Hawaiian moonshine that he kept in a pint flask. Prohibition was in effect until March of 1933, and even then, there were many regulations needed to dispense liquor. For being drunk and disorderly he received a suspended sentence of 13 months. Also, while in Hawaii, on February 10, Ace met a ship carrying fellow boxers, "Baby" Tiger Flowers, and JJ Moose Tausig. On February 13, Ace was scheduled to workout at Sato's Gym, but did not show. On July 17, there were more charges of drunk driving when he almost crashed into a gas station. In the summer of 1933, Ace had a nose job because he said, *"I may go in for a motion picture career."*

"Ace Hudkins Tosses Punches In Café And Stops Bullets", *"Ace Hudkins Takes It from Gun In Midriff"*, and *"Ace Hudkins Shot Twice During L.A. Beer Parlor Brawl"*, were some of the headlines on August 7, 1933, when Ace was shot. According to newspaper reports, he had entered the bar with some friends and became belligerent, throwing punches, threatening to shoot out the lights, and to *"show you how to run your place."* The barkeep, Mr. Harris, said, *"You can't do that Ace... Stop beating up people in the place,"* and

asked him to leave. When Ace refused, and began taking out an empty pistol, the barkeep fired two shots: one into his right lung, which ended up lodged in his pelvis, and the other, which had been headed for his heart, was deflected by a rib. There were even articles which sounded more like obituaries, such as *Mile-Posts In The Life Of A Nebraska Wildcat.* They had written Ace off, but Ace had been under-estimated before and fought back. Ace's mother, Mary, his brothers, Fon and Oraine, and a nephew, Leonard, came to his Glendale Hospital bedside from Nebraska. Ace received two transfusions. *"Ace Hudkins Wins Fight With Death"*, *"Ace Hudkins Wins Bout With Grim Reaper"*, and *"Ace Hudkins Wins Battle For Life"*, were some of the triumphant headlines on August 11 and 12.

After out-fighting King Levinsky on July 1, 1931, Ace was re-energized and went on to beat Chuck Burns on July 15, 1931. Ace won the California Heavyweight Title from Dynamite Jackson on September 15, 1931, then had it taken away by young Lee Ramage on February 23, 1932. It was really the fight against Wesley Ketchel at the Olympic Auditorium on November 29, 1932 that made him decide to hang up the gloves. Ace remembered, *"This was it. I had finally gotten hurt- three broken ribs. I knew I had had it."*

True Champs

Not All Topnotchers Are Accorded Recognition They've Earned In The Prize Ring And Elsewhere

By Damon Runyon

We got in a big argument the other night with a fellow who said that the prize fighter could not be rated truly great unless he became a champion. We told him that was like saying a man could not be rated a truly great man unless he became president when everybody knows that we have had many men in the history of this country who never became president yet were greater than any president who ever lived.

...we have known quite a number of prizefighters who were truly great fighters, probably greater than any champions, but who never became champions because of lack of opportunity or the way the pugilistic cards were stacked against them.

Ace Hudkins was a blond thunderbolt in his heyday...His one thought was to get at his opponent and tear him to pieces. Ace fought as a lightweight, welterweight and middleweight and, though never a champion, he could lick 99 percent of the guys who thought they were champions. Between them, [Buddy] Taylor and Hudkins probably drew more money in a year than all the present champions put together, bar Joe Lois.

Runyon, Damon. "True Champs" *The Evening Review* (East Liverpool, Ohio) 10 June, 1942, Wed. Page 4

In 1932, at a mere 27 years old, a certain friend of Ace's and a fellow California transplant from Nebraska, Darry F. Zanuck no less, encouraged Ace to enter the movie business in an unexpected way. Ace, along with brothers Clyde and Art would raise horses at the Hudkins Bros. Movie Ranch. Their horses would be in some of the best Westerns at the time when Westerns ruled the theaters. John Wayne, Roy Rogers, William Holden, Glenn Ford, James Cagney and Nebraskan, Ward Bond were among only a few who would be acquainted with the Hudkins and their four-legged friends…

Rich Brehm, son of stuntman John Brehm, and nephew to Ace, through Marie (Sader) Brehm, recollects Ace at the ranch in the late '30's. *"I remember when we come out from Nebraska, I think it was '37, to California, they still had a ring out there at the ranch or this property that they leased. They had a regular ring out there set up underneath a big old tree. I remember Ace getting up there and starting to warm up. Joe Lewis was coming up as the heavyweight there at that time, and Ace thought he could whip him, but it never materialized. So, I never did see him fight and everything. But I heard all about it. I know when he would get drunk and come up there to the ranch, everybody'd clear out. But we never had no problems. I was just a little kid then."*

On July7, 1949, at 43 years old, Ace was brought before the judge on drunk driving charges. He was fined $135.00, ordered to attend Alcoholics Anonymous, and not to drive for a year.

In the later part of Ace's life, he had settled down tremendously. This could be attributed to age and maturity but, then again, this author likes to think that it was also due to the calming influence of Mildred Herron, Ace's true love of his life. Milded doted on Ace and her love calmed him down. She created scrapbooks for him, all about his career. The information in these scrapbooks provided much of the color for this book. No more did he feel the need to take risks and drive intoxicated, or get into bar fights. He didn't have to be "The Wildcat" 24 hours a day. He could relax. He could focus on horse racing, and "The Ranch" as it was known in the family. Ace and Mildred travelled the country following the horse races, and enjoying life.

Ace also enjoyed spending time with nephew Acey Hudkins, Clyde's son, and Clyde and Gene Sader, Clyde's nephews.

When asked in his later years what he thought of the new generation of boxers, Ace said this, *"Boxers nowadays don't train hard enough. Once around the block in road work and they think they are ready to go. Also, they've too many other interests. It's hard work and a fighter has to be ready for a peak effort every time."*

In 1961, journalist George Baker wrote, *"Just go up to the Ace and tell him he was a puffed-up fighter who never was champ because he never really had it. Go ahead! Chances are you'll find yourself staring at the sky- after you wake up from a visitation from the horny fist of the 55-year-old rancher who was once the most savage, animalistic brawler in the ring. He's still the Ace."*

Ace passed away at Hollywood Presbyterian Hospital on April 17, 1973 of complications from Parkinson's Disease. Many family members, including the author's mother, Jean, and father, Gene, gathered at the hospital. The great "Wildcat" of the ring was finally at rest. He was 67 and he had outlived his brothers.

Dr. Willliam Branch stated that Ace *"had just plain wore out."*

Ace rests beside his brothers at Grand View Memorial Park in Glendale, California. Side by side as they always had been.

But that is not the end of Ace's story -- not by a long shot! For as long as tales are told, and memories shared, Ace will always be with us. And there are many more stories to share. Stories about the ranch, Trigger, and Robin Hood. Stories from James Drury, Denny Miller, and Clint Walker, among others. Stories about cowboys, stuntmen, Hollywood heroes and Hollywood bad boys.

There are many more stories waiting to be told-- and they will be...

113 Ace's resting place at Grandview. (findagrave.com)

Do Your Stuff

Do your stuff- and let 'em beller,

Do your best and let 'em rap,

If you win, they'd holler "Lucky":

If you lose, they'd holler "Sap":

Let 'em help or let 'em hinder,

You should worry - do your stuff,

You're the guy you have to live with,

Be yourself, and treat 'em rough.

From Ace Hudkins Scrapbook

Acknowledgments

A book, any book, but especially a biography, is never written alone. There is research and support that is needed. I could not have written this book without many people helping me along the way. First, I would like to thank God from Whom all blessings flow. If I didn't have Him, I would have nothing.

Thank you especially to my mom. You are the best person I know, and you have supported me through life's journey every step of the way. You have read my notes, helped me to choose photos, and been a great friend in a million ways.

Thank you, dad. My dad passed away while I was in the middle of research for this book, so he didn't get to see his uncle Ace's story in print.

Thank you, Jen Rose. It was due to your contribution that the LAPL photos are included. Thanks for always asking how the book was coming and being willing to listen or to look up information for me. You are the true definition of "friend".

Thank you, Jill Merle, from Little Red Lines. Your suggestions always made the writing stronger. You are a terrific editor, and I couldn't have finished this book without you.

Thank you, Lana Hudkins for your support and generous gift of Ace's scrapbooks.

Thank you Gene LeBell, for being generous with your time and information.

Thank you to the following libraries: Los Angeles Public Library, UCLA, USC, Notre Dame, UNLV. Thank you to Douglas Cavanaugh, Hollywood Legion Stadium, and all the great people I have met on Facebook. I used Newspapers.com, BoxRec.com and Ancestry.com extensively for research. Thank you to all my friends and supporters. It means the world to me.

Date	Opponent	Location	Result
1932-11-29	Wesley Ketchell	Olympic Auditorium, Los Angeles	Loss (P)
1932-02-23	Lee Ramage	Olympic Auditorium, Los Angeles USA California State Heavyweight Title	Loss (UD)
1931-09-15	Dynamite Jackson	Olympic Auditorium, Los Angeles USA California State Heavyweight Title	Win (P)
1931-07-15	Chuck Burns	Detroit	Win (TKO)
1931-07-01	King Levinsky	Mills Stadium, Chicago	Win (P)
1930-08-26	Jack McVey	Olympic Auditorium, Los Angeles	N C
1930-05-27	Dave Shade	Olympic Auditorium, Los Angeles	Loss (P)
1930-02-14	Maxie Rosenbloom	Madison Square Garden, New York	Loss (UD)
1930-01-31	Arthur Flynn	Boston Gardens, Boston	Win (KO)

Date	Opponent	Location	Result
1929-10-29	Mickey Walker	Wrigley Field, Los Angeles	Loss (P)
1929-09-24	Joe Anderson	Olympic Auditorium, Los Angeles	Win (RTD)
1929-06-28	Charley Belanger	Dreamland Auditorium, San Francisco	Win (P)
1929-05-24	Tom Moore	Legion Stadium, Hollywood	Win (TKO)
1929-04-15	Armand Emanuel	Wrigley Field, Los Angeles	Win (P)
1928-12-28	Rene De Vos	Madison Square Garden, New York	Win (MD)
Date	Opponent	Location	Result
1928-10-02	Joe Anderson	Olympic Auditorium, Los Angeles	Loss (P)
1928-06-21	Mickey Walker	Comisky Park, Chicago	Loss (SD)
1928-06-05	Buck Holley	Landis Field Arena, Lincoln	Win (TKO)
1928-05-22	Billy Lane	Armory, Portand	Win (KO)
1928-02-27	Al Mello	Arena, Boston	Win (DQ)
1928-02-17	Sergeant Sammy Baker	Madison Square Garden, New York	Win (P)
1928-01-20	Lew Tendler	Madison Square Garden, New York	Win (UD)
1928-01-06	Mike Rozgall	City Auditorium, Omaha	Win (TKO)
1927-11-29	Herman Auerbach	Olympic Auditorium, Los Angeles	Win (RTD)
1927-09-16	Arizona Joe Rivers	Phoenix	Win (KO)
1927-07-25	Sergeant Sammy Baker	Wrigley Field, Los Angeles	Win (P)
1927-06-	Sergeant	Polo Grounds, New	Lose

15	Sammy Baker	York	(TKO)
1927-06-01	Al Mello	Queensboro Stadium, Long island City, Queens	Win (P)
1927-04-22	Sid Socklyn	Legion Stadium, Hollywood	Win (TKO)
1927-04-12	Lew Tendler	Olympic Auditorium, Los Angeles	Win (P)
1927-03-08	Bert Colima	Wrigley Field, Los Angeles	Win (P)

Date	Opponent	Location	Result
1927-02-15	Billy Arkinson	Olympic Auditorium, Los Angeles	Win (TKO)
1927-02-01	Billy Alger	Olympic Auditorium, Los Angeles	Win (P)
1927-01-10	Pat Corbett	Univ. of Nebraska, Fieldhouse Coliseum, Lincoln	Win (P)
1926-10-29	Phil McGraw	Madison Square Garden, New York	Win (P)
1926-08-27	Phil McGraw	Coney Island Stadium, Brooklyn	Win
1926-08-06	Stanislaus Loayza	Coney Island Stadium, Brooklyn	Drawn-points
1926-06-25	Ruby Goldstein	Coney Island Stadium, Brooklyn	Win (KO)
1926-06-24	Phil Salvadore	Legion Stadium, Hollywood	Win (TKO)
1926-05-26	Tommy O'Brien	Olympic Auditorium, Los Angeles	Drawn-points
1926-04-14	Johnny Adams	Olympic Auditorium, Los Angeles	Lose (P)
1926-03-12	Sammy Santos	Coliseum, San Diego	Win (P)

Date	Opponent	Location	Result
1926-03-05	Johnny Lamar	Legion Stadium, Hollywood	Win (P)
1926-02-17	Tommy O'Brien	Olympic Auditorium, Los Angeles	Lose (P)
1926-01-22	Frankie Schaeffer	Legion Stadium, Hollywood	Win (P)
1925-11-14	Mushy Callahan	Maier Park, Vernon, California	Lose (P)
1925-11-06	Johnny O'Donnell	Legion Stadium, Hollywood	Win (P)
1925-10-21	Mike Ballerino	Olympic Auditorium, Los Angeles	Win (P)
1925-09-16	Mushy Callahan	Olympic Auditorium, Los Angeles	Draw (P)
1925-09-04	Dick Hoppe	Legion Stadium, Hollywood	Win (P)
1925-08-11	Lou Paluso	Arena, Vernon, California	Draw (P)
Date	Opponent	Location	Result
1925-07-10	Sid Terris	East Chicago	Lose (Newspaper Decision)
1925-06-06	Tommy O'Brien	Ascot Park, Los Angeles	Lose (DQ)
1925-04-07	Joe Benjamin	Arena, Vernon, California	Win (P)
1925-03-07	Frank Barrett	Lyceum A.C., Los Angeles	Win (P)
1925-02-27	Pat Mills	Legion Stadium, Hollywood	Win (P)
1925-02-06	Spug Myers	Legion Stadium, Hollywood	Win (P)
1925-01-09	Tommy Carter	Legion Stadium, Hollywood	Win (P)
1924-12-19	Dick Hoppe	Legion Stadium, Hollywood	Win (P)

1924-11-28	Frankie Schaeffer	East Chicago	Win (Newspaper Decision)
1924-11-24	Russie LeRoy	Auditorium, Sioux City	Lose (Newspaper Decision)
1924-11-14	Frankie Schaeffer	East Chicago	Win (Newspaper Decision)
1924-11-07	Johnny O'Donnell	Auditorium, Omaha	Win (P)

Date	Opponent	Location	Result
1924-10-24	Frankie Schaeffer	East Chicago	Lose (Newspaper Decision
1924-09-19	Sammy Leonard	Auditorium, Omaha	Lose (DQ)
1924-09-04	Kid Worley	City Auditorium, Lincoln, Neb., USA Nebraska State Lightweight Title	Win (TKO)
1924-08-29	Russie LeRoy	Mizzou Park, Sioux City	Lose (Newspaper Decision)
1924-08-20	Ever Hammer	City Auditorium, Omaha	Win (DQ)
1924-07-21	Eddie DeBeau	Mizzou Park, Sioux City	Win (Newspaper Decision)
1924-07-01	Eddie McCarthy	Elks Lodge, McCook, Neb.	Win (P)
1924-06-26	Reddy Blanchard	Omaha	Win (TKO)
1924-05-27	Battling Strayer	City Auditorium, Lincoln	Win (TKO)

Date	Opponent	Location	Result
1924-05-24	Si Sandage	Cudahy Recreation Hall, Sioux City	Win (KO)
1924-05-14	Frankie Dean	Omaha	Win (P)

Date	Opponent	Location	Result
1924-05-07	Jack Zalice	Des Moines	Win (Newspaper Decision)
1924-03-25	Erwin Bige	City Auditorium, Lincoln, USA Nebraska State Lightweight Title	Win (P)
1924-03-17	Jack O'Toole	Omaha	Win (P)
1924-02-29	Rusty Jones	City Auditorium, Omaha	Win (KO)
1924-02-12	Battling Strayer	City Auditorium, Lincoln, USA Nebraska State Lightweight Title	Win (P)
1924-01-22	Bobby Slater	City Auditorium, Lincoln	Win (KO)
1924-01-18	Erwin Bige	Omaha	Draw (P)
1923-12-14	Johnny Harris	Cudahy, A.C., South Omaha	Win (KO)
1923-12-08	Harry LaBarre	Cudahy Recreation Hall, Sioux City	Draw (Newspaper Decision)
1923-11-07	Buddy Chambers	City Auditorium, Omaha	Win (P)
1923-10-19	Harold Plude	Cudahy, A.C. Omaha	Draw (P)
1923-09-20	Sailor Larsen	York, Nebraska	Win (KO)

Date	Opponent	Location	Result
1923-09-06	Len Schwabel	Landis Field, Lincoln	Win (P)
1923-08-24	Rusty Evans	Central City, Nebraska	Win (KO)
1923-07-04	Al Dale	Bridgeport, Nebraska	Win (P)
Date	Opponent	Location	Result
1923-06-08	Stubby Morse	Alliance, Nebraska	Win (KO)
1923-04-27	Johnny Harris	City Auditorium, Lincoln	Draw (P)
1923-04-18	Rusty Evans	Elks Lodge, York, Neb.	Draw (P)
1923-04-10	Harold Jelsma	Lincoln Hotel, Lincoln	Draw (P)
1923-02-21	Kid Worley	Grand Island, Nebraska	Lose (P)
1923-01-19	Kid Worley	Grand Island, Nebraska	Draw (P)
1923-01-12	Erwin Bige	City Auditorium, Omaha	Lose (P)
1922-12-29	Eddie Ferris	Cudahy A.C. South Omaha	Win (KO)
1922-11-11	Bud Hamilton	Alliance, Nebraska	Draw (P)
1922-06-02	Frank Conley	Harlan, Nebraska	Win (KO)
1922-05-15	Speed Springer	Wahoo, Nebraska	Lose (P)
1922-04-19	Harold Jelsma	Tecumseh, Nebraska	Win (P)
1922-03-10	Harold Jelsma	Lincoln A.C., Lincoln, Nebraska	Draw (P)

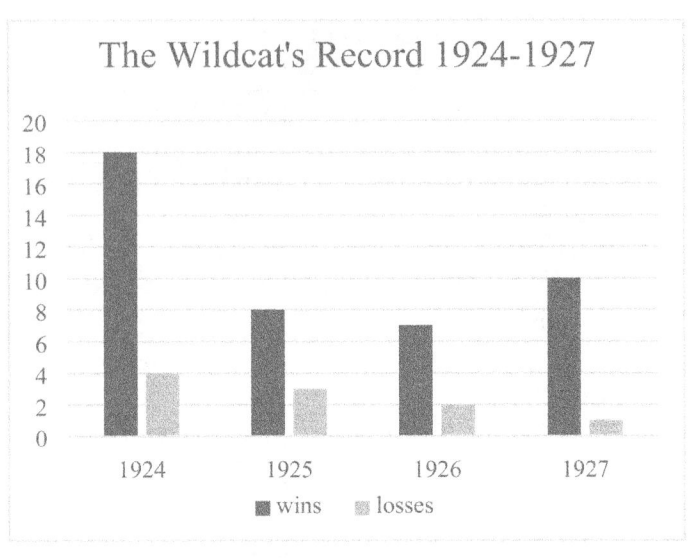

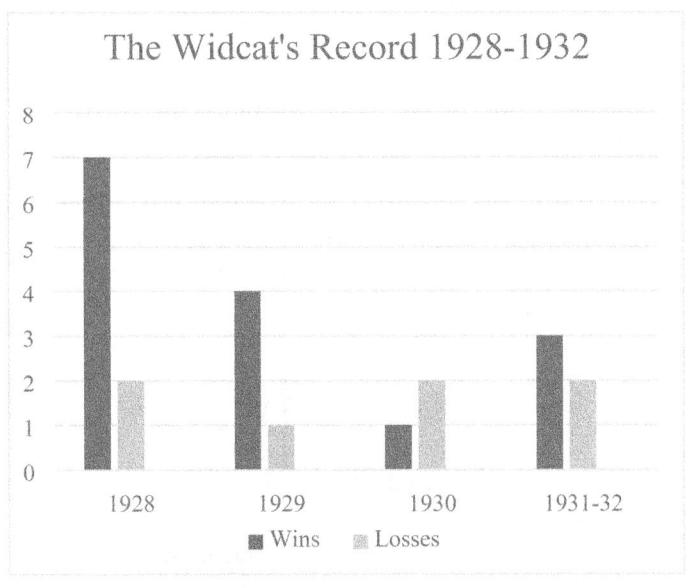

Bibliography

Newspaper articles in chronological order.

Nebraska State Journal, November 12, 1893

The North Platte Semi-Weekly Tribune (North Platte, Nebraska) Friday, Oct 19, 1900.

Lincoln Journal Star, (Lincoln, Nebraska) 02 June 1915 Wed

The Lincoln Star (Lincoln, Nebraska) 21 July 1920, Wednesday

The Lincoln Star, (Lincoln, Neb) 19 Mar 1925 Th.

Edgren, Robert. "Conceit makes Fortunes For 'Ace' Hudkins: Huge crowd attracted by his ring antics." *The Des Moines Register,* (Des Moines, Iowa) 20 October 1925 Tues. Page 12

The Nebraska State Journal (Lincoln, Nebraska) Sun, Feb 7, 1926

Los Angeles Times, April 11, 1926

Lincoln Evening Journal (Lincoln, Nebraska) 03, August 1926

The Nebraska State Journal (Lincoln, Nebraska) 11 Jan 1927, Tues., Page 6

The Morning Call (Allentown, Pennsylvania) Wed, June 15, 1927 Page 20

Cauliflower Alley Notes, Los Angeles Paper – July 1927 Ace's scrapbook

Self Defense Magazine (New York, NY) July 1927

The Los Angeles Referee October 1927

The Lincoln Star (Lincoln, Nebraska) 27 June 1928, Wed

The Los Angeles Times (Los Angeles, California) Thu, July 5, 1928 Page 14

Farrell, Henry L. "Hooks and Slides" *The Daily Tribune* (Wisconsin Rapids, Wisconsin) 27 Dec. 1928, Thu., page 5.

Roche, Frank. "Meet the Nebraska Wildcat!" *The Arena* Oct 10, 1929: 14-15, 35, 36

The Times (Munster, Indiana) 22 Oct. 1929, Tues, Main Edition, page 20

The Los Angeles Times (Los Angeles, California) Tue, Oct 29, 1929 Page 37

Oakland Tribune (Oakland, California) Tue, Oct 29, 1929 Page 30

The San Bernardino County Sun (San Bernardino, California) Tues. Oct 29, 1929 Page 14

Lincoln Star Journal (Lincoln, Nebraska) 05 Jan 1932

The Mansfield Journal (Mansfield, Ohio) 04 Aug 1932 Th. Page 13

Lincoln Star Journal (Lincoln, Nebraska) 07 August 1933 Monday page 9

Runyon, Damon. "True Champs" *The Evening Review* (East Liverpool, Ohio) 10 June 1942, Wed. Page 4

The Ottawa Journal (Ottawa, Ontario, Canada) Wed, Feb 22, 1950 page 19

Raglin, Jim. "Ace Hudkins Named to Nebraska Sports Hall of Fame." *Lincoln Evening Journal*, (Lincoln, Nebraska) 09 Aug 1955, Page 11

Baker, George. "Ace Hudkins Had The Face Of a Killer." *Boxing Illustrated: The Magazine For Ring Fans*. Mar. 1961: pgs. 18,19,62, 63, 65

"Fight Game was Good to Ace Hudkins." *The Los Angeles Times,* (Los Angeles, California) 05 Mar. 1961

Springer, Steve. "The City was Full of Fight." *The Los Angeles Times*. Mar. 30, 2006.

http://www.latimes.com/sports/la-sp-125boxingmar30-story.html

Books

Willa Cather, My Antonia, (Everyman's Library, New York, 1996) 18

Brehm, Richard Interview 2004

Cohen, E. a. (2005). *Brother Men: The Correspondence of Edgar Rice Burroughs and Herbert T. Weston.* Duke University Press.

Interviews

Brehm, Richard Interview 2004

LeBell, Gene Interview 2012

Additional Websites

https://www.brainyquote.com/authors/muhammad_ali

http://www.boxing.com/when_jack_kearns_saved_the_bulldogs_bacon.html

Special photos:

Film transparency of Ace Hudkins posing with men, Las Vegas, 1929 pg. 231
Ulloms (photo studio);
University of Nevada, Las Vegas University Libraries 1929
Image ID: 0265 0256

Film transparency of Ace Hudkins, Las Vegas, 1929 pg.234
Ulloms (photo studio);
University of Nevada, Las Vegas University Libraries 1929
Image ID: 0265 0258

Film transparency of Ace Hudkins, Las Vegas, 1929 pg. 235
Ulloms (photo studio);
University of Nevada, Las Vegas University Libraries 1929
Image ID: 0265 0259

Cover Photo
Ace Hudkins, Boxer
Los Angeles Public Library
Los Angeles Herald-Examiner Collection Photographs
Order Number: 00030131

Sharkey and Hudkins pg. 173
Los Angeles Public Library
Los Angeles Herald-Examiner Collection Photographs
Order Number: 00054092
Location HE Box 1707

Ace Hudkins — half length portrait as boxer [14 May 1925]. pg. 57
University of Notre Dame Hesburgh Libraries
Rare Books and Special Collections
Harry E. Winkler Collection of Boxing Photographs
710-15-33

Ace Hudkins (left, hand being wrapped) and Clyde Hudkins — three-quarter length portraits, in ring. pg. 180
University of Notre Dame Hesburgh Libraries
Rare Books and Special Collections

Harry E. Winkler Collection of Boxing Photographs
710-15-80

Ace Hudkins, Southern California, 1927 pg. 165
Dick Whittington Studio 1927
University of Southern California Libraries
Dick Whittington Photography Collection 1924-1987
File name: DW-1927-73-14-60
http://digitallibrary.usc.edu/cdm/compoundobject/collection/p15799coll170/id/74082/rec/9

Ace Hudkins, Southern California, 1927 pg. 166
Dick Whittington Studio 1927
University of Southern California Libraries
Dick Whittington Photography Collection 1924-1987
File name: DW-1927-03-14-60
http://digitallibrary.usc.edu/cdm/compoundobject/collection/p15799coll170/id/26250/rec/1

Boxer Ace Hudkins, Posing 1927 pg. 131
P&A Photos 1927
University of California, Los Angeles Library
Los Angeles Times Photographic Archive, Department of Special Collections,
Charles E. Young Research Library
edu.ucla.library.specialCollections.latimes:8143, uclamss_1429_9670

Boxer Ace Hudkins, Posing 1927 pg. 132

P&A Photos 1927

University of California, Los Angeles Library

Los Angeles Times Photographic Archive, Department of Special Collections,

Charles E. Young Research Library

edu.ucla.library.specialCollections.latimes:8144, uclamss_1429_9671

Ace Hudkins and Mickey Walker pg. 197

Associated Press

October 26, 1929

ID: 291026023

http://www.apimages.com/metadata/Index/Watchf-AP-S-BOX-CA-USA-APHS427678-Ace-Hudkins/e12805a162f248aeb46d65984c85dc1c/5/0

www.ingramcontent.com/pod-product-compliance
Lightning Source LLC
Chambersburg PA
CBHW060112170426
43198CB00010B/865